CRANIAL BUNKER

ALSO BY STEPHEN OLIVER

Henwise (1975)
& interviews (1978)
Autumn Songs (1978)
Letter To James K. Baxter (1980)
Earthbound Mirrors (1984)
Guardians, Not Angels (1993)
Islands of Wilderness—A Romance (1996)
Unmanned (1999)
Election Year Blues (1999)
Night of Warehouses: Poems 1978-2000 (2001)
Deadly Pollen (2003)
Ballads, Satire & Salt—A Book of Diversions (2003)
Either Side The Horizon (2005)
Parable Of The Sea Sponge (2007)
Harmonic (2008)
Apocrypha (2010)
Intercolonial (2013)
Gone: Satirical Poems: New & Selected (2016)
Luxembourg (2018)
Heroides / 15 Sonnets (2020)
The Song Of Globule / 80 Sonnets (2020)

Prose
Unposted, Autumn Leaves / A Memoir In Essays (2021)

CRANIAL BUNKER

POEMS BY

STEPHEN OLIVER

GP
GREYWACKE PRESS
LAT. 25°/50° SOUTH. LONG. 145°/180° EAST

First published 2023

Greywacke Press
9 Lynch St
Hughes
ACT 2605
Australia
reid1801@bigpond.com
greywackepress@gmail.com

Oliver, Stephen 1950-
Title: Cranial Bunker
ISBN 978-0-646-87333-6

Cover design composed by Stephen Oliver
Cover photo of author: Allan MacGillivray

Affinity formatting by John Denny
of Puriri Press, Auckland

A catalogue record for this book is available from the
National Library of Australia

© Stephen Oliver

All rights reserved.
No part of this publication may be reproduced, stored in a retrieval system,
or transmitted in any form or by any means, electronic, mechanical,
photocopying, scanning, recording or otherwise, without the prior permission
of the copyright owner.

ACKNOWLEDGEMENTS

The Blue Nib Magazine (Ireland); *The Canberra Times* (Australia); *InDaily* (Australia); *The Daily Breaking News-TDBN* (USA); *The Leipzig Glocal* (Germany); *London Grip* (UK); *Love In The Time Of COVID: A Chronicle Of A Pandemic* (NZ); *Ngā Kupu Waikato: Anthology of Waikato Poetry* 2019 (NZ); *The Palestine Chronicle* (USA); *Poetry New Zealand Yearbook* 2019; *Poetry New Zealand Yearbook* 2021; *The Ultimate Reader Of Love For The Book: Anthology* (NZ); *Verity La* (Australia).

The prose poem, *Vive La Sans-Dents*, shortlisted for the *Fair Australia Poetry Prize* 2019.

The poem, *Fig Tree*, first appeared in *Unposted, Autumn Leaves / A Memoir In Essays* by Stephen Oliver, Greywacke Press, Canberra 2021.

Special thanks to Dr. Heinz Leonhard (Leo) Kretzenbacher, School of Languages and Linguistics, German Studies Program, University of Melbourne, for his translation into German of my commemorative prose poem, *That Farther Shore*, for Rudi Krausmann.

'The wick is the glowworm of the lamp'
—Isidore of Seville: *The Etymologies*

CONTENTS

PALIMPSEST	3
ECLOGUE	6
POPLARS	7
BATTLE OF TOLLENSE	8
ARROWHEADS	10
MANIFEST	12
BANISHMENT	13
VISITANT	14
VIEWING PLATFORM	15
SHALLOW CREEK	16
FACTORY TOWN	18
WHISTLING	19
LAST WORDS	20
THE ARTIFICIAL FLOWER	21
PERIPLUS	23
THE OTHER SIDE	24
THE LITERALIST	25
VIVE LA SANS-DENTS	26
THE MIGRATION	27
ANALYTICS	30
CHERT	32
LADY OF THE MURALS	33
STAMP MILL	34
OTHERWISE	35
THE BRASHER DOUBLOON (1947)	36
SIREN CITY	37
DON'T BE ALARMED	38
STEPS	39
GO THE DISTANCE	40
THE COMMON GOOD	41
BIG DATA	42
WAY OF LIFE	43
SCAFFOLDING	44
TO WHAT?	45
DISTANT	46

PREFACE TO A FOREST	47
CRANIAL BUNKER	48
FOREST OF STARS	50
THAT FARTHER SHORE	51
THE POLITICIAN	53
ANTHONY KINGSMILL-LUNN (1926-1993)	54
FIG TREE	55
TENT FLAP	56
EPIGRAMS FOR THE DISENCHANTED	58
WELCOME GHOST	77
SWING BRIDGE	80
UNWRITTEN	81
THE CARETAKER	83
WHAT LIES AHEAD	84
RUIN	86
SHUTTERS	87
THE PRINTER	89
DIGITAL GHOSTS	90
FARTHER OFF	91
LOOKOUT	92
COMPASS	93
BURN DOWN THE AMAZON	94
FANDANGO	95
OBLIGATORY	96
YOU SEE IT	97
GRAND TOUR	100
GRID	101
FAR OFF	102
DEAD RINGER	103
SHE WATCHES	104
TREMORS	105
OSSUARY	106
REBRANDED FREEDOM	107
ENACTED ELSEWHERE	108
PHANTOMS	109
LONG SINCE ENDED	110
DUCK ISLAND	111

CRANIAL BUNKER

PALIMPSEST

You arrive in Paris in 1902, as did Rilke,
age 26: great cities are the sum of all that will
happen to them, and like the weather,
omnipresent, that which will occur has, and the
past retreats into the future; clouds clog
the horizon, rise to vast, domed cupola upon
which you can project your own slide show;
the comings and goings, incidents unfold into
histories, the invading forces through the Arc de
Triomphe; Celan tumbles into the Seine,
Gérard de Nerval hangs from the grille 'in the
darkest street he could find', the Rue de la
Vieille-Lanterne; the myriad blank canvases ranged
along the Left Bank, like an endless procession
of days, waiting to be painted, to remake
Paris over and over. It is true, 'great cities are the
sum of all that will happen to them', palimpsest
of memory, that is little more than filtered
twilight; the child rings his bell, the red balloon
floats over mansard rooftops, *'where narrow streets
bend proudly to the stars'* [1] past the splayed,
iron petticoats of the Eiffel Tower; past & present,
an espalier of metaphor, woven through this
City of Lights, these blown banners of the ages.

                History is a slaughterhouse
preserved as museum. O it is Easter in downtown
Warsaw, and the Poles are whooping it
up nearby, consciously oblivious of the ghetto's
plea bargaining with the Lord, cries that
become silent film footage, flickering in the corpse
light. Hear how guilt congeals to anger
and accusation decades hence. We are heroes.
We are victims, book-ended between East and West.
We rode our horses against the German tanks,
'my rifle, my saddle, and me'. 'We suffered

countless incursions across our borders.'
Olga Tokarczuk, courageous, prized open the lid
of National Pride, to expose the hypocrisy.
'Slave-owners. Colonizers. Murderers of Jews',
only to have the ghouls turn, maliciously, against her.
History is a mass grave weighted down by
Public Monuments, a shroud stitched through with
anthems along the appliqué of Nationalism.
The shuffling steps of the refugees haunt their day
dreams. And finally, when dream has defeated
memory, it is safe to come out and stare at the rain
shiny curb; the brick walls weighty with a
mediaeval pageant of light, sodden, that blocks out
the heavy steps of the slowly dissolving armies.

A shunted siding of words brought to a halt
with an expletive, or begun with one. All those
light-fuelled days of remembered warmth
gone, dull as varnish. "I want two bodies, one face
down one belly up", shouts the director, "use the
fat extras". He's a Gung Ho, 'Hell Yeah!'
sort of guy, this is a Gulf War movie, "they'll look
bloated," he says. A movie shot down Louisiana
way amongst the cottonwoods and bayou.
He leans on an old tree trunk, sees a horse's head
in the bark. He makes a mental note that every
foreign conflict his country wages is a subconscious
rerun of the American Civil War. Night has
fallen back at the trailer, the movie's going nowhere
fast, but the plasma screen comes to the rescue.
The Eiffel Tower looms black as an obelisk
in the night, the lights of Paris dimmed to campfires,
flickering spasms of pain, the staggered glow.
Men in black tactical gear, the aggrandizement
in lockdown. Bodies, the rubble-strewn restaurant.
Shot, she survived—only later to tell the media,
'As I lay down in the blood of strangers ...' [2]
that she thought of all those she loved, drawing their
faces close round her, as she prayed, and bodies
fell, as finally gunfire ceased amidst the screams.

December 2015

[1] *'where narrow streets bend proudly to the stars'*—Hope Mirrlees / Paris (1919)

[2] *'As I lay down in the blood of strangers ...'*—Isobel Bowdery, Paris attack survivor, Friday 13, November 2015

ECLOGUE

The sign read, Hora Hora, more district
than place, maybe a community hall nearby, the
hydro village long since drowned under
Lake Karapiro. Farther up into hill country
(the lake now lost to view) hydrangeas glowed
white along some farmstead driveway,
beneath overarching, dark green elms. Stillness.
Back at the lake, quad skis relentlessly
swung back and forth, in front of Hora Hora
Public Domain, rodeos on waterways.

                    Grain silos rustling at Walton,
wind gusts awash through trees—then
the small, humpback bridge, across the railway
line, by the red brick Community Church.
In the foreground, a corrugated iron roof folds
over like a badly parted hairdo, barn style.
Poplars all in a row, waiting for wind to make
an impression. By the time it takes to reach
Kiwitahi School, you've guessed that, whatever
it was, has gone back underground. A Ute
pulls past, by Eureka Hall, the settlement now
receding, as though you had exited a portal
into what must be an embodiment of the present,
grain silos, railway bridge, white hydrangeas.

POPLARS

Tikitiki Road, Aramatai, Waikato

A phalanx of poplars further on
into Tikitiki Road, crouching lions,
pursued by tusks of shadow,
cutting between. Early autumn, March.
"Sheep country?" I heard myself ask
in the otherwise light. And the
avenue of poplars either side of this
unsealed road, facing off
like bronze warriors; then becoming
bison, watering.

      Poplars, impressionistic
visitants, sweeping through the seasons.
Here, a scatter of leaves, gilded
offerings made to the valley gods from
these back country sentinels.
The avenue bolt straight, while in
the foreground bison bend golden heads,
in procession. The farmer on his
quad bike unhurriedly gone. "Back with
a tractor," he said. Nearby, off
the dirt road up ahead, dogs chorused,
reverberated, seemingly distant.

BATTLE OF TOLLENSE

Europe's Oldest Known Battlefield

Tollense River, 1250 BC, Bronze Age,
a small, marshy valley. Cloud, hack silvered.
Sparsely populated, in what is now
north-eastern Germany; no villages or towns.
The siege of Troy had not yet occurred,
lay one hundred years distant.

                Only the loose
confederation of extended, family farms
homaged to an emergent warrior class;
professional soldiers from far-flung forests,
from as far away as Nova Scotia
spruce, or by way of the steppes, too, but
maybe that was rumoured.

                And there by the
winding Tollense River that flows toward
the Baltic Sea (its course unchanged
for millennia), bones of the war-weary dead.
Flint, bronze arrowheads, arm rings
and axe heads, mallets of blackthorn,
clubs made from ash, found mud mangled
and buried in the swale.

                4,000 men clashed
by the bridge along a three kilometre strip in
hand-to-hand, clamorous combat.
Horses and men fell, hundreds lay dead
or dying. Bodies sank in shallow, peaty pools,
some plundered for booty, others tossed
into the Tollense.

Before the act,
before the atrocity, was there stillness?
Not the mind's dull echo, after the slaughter,
when defeat and victory copulated;
the shock of realization—but that other
stillness, spears sharply defined
against the skyline (later recalled in song).
How forest light transfixed the valley,
made of the river a silver scroll.

              Dry rasp of leather,
breath suspended, this now a treasured
thought, the moment hallucinogenic;
senses heightened, vision manifest, clear.
The arrow taut on the bowstring
an instant before release, objects and men,
outlined in an otherworldly aura—
the flung shadow of the first spear cast.

ARROWHEADS

That burning tree, the perfect touch
down into autumn, leaves, a high tensile
blue at dusk, buckling to orange;
tempered darkness struck through, the
living become memories of the dead.
Conjuring halls and bedchambers,
an age of saddle horses and war horses.
A yellow blade slants from one lit
window, elongates patio, bleeds shadow
darkly, as blue becomes an opaque
blanket rising into night. Autumn exposes,
once again, nests from newly forgot
seasons, beneath those trees cut
with copper foil. Birds work the branch
networks, parcels of song swapped
in the half-light. Cloud pelts shaken out
before an inhaling moon, near full,
over leaves cast into a scattering of bent
arrowheads. The air chill, chugging
with bird call. A dull, clapperboard sound,
wind gusts, rain hitting trees, that
far off fugue on Orini Downs—from
Maungakawa Reserve, a stitched, tree-skin
cloak flung over Maungatautari, seams
thick along its flank. Windbreaks, copses,
falling away in an orderly fashion
out across the Hauraki Plains—squat
bungalows, crouched into the hills behind,
overlooking cloud and light flooded
lowlands. Back here in suburbia,
a half-submerged skylight, one sunken
moon, air slate grey as roof tiles.
Come morning, I will make my escape
from box canyon, head South on the
Waikato Expressway, skirt Cambridge

with its genteel stud farms, country
estates, wind my way up Sanatorium Hill.
Some morning, when those heights
turn heavy-sleeved and baggy with fog,
and rusted roofs redden to autumn.

MANIFEST

There was always doubt that lay indestructible upon the horizon, distant and beautiful in its formlessness, that appeared to be slowly massing but gave no indication of immediate danger. Disturbed and silent as mime yet still too far away to engage us, for it seemed to be a living thing. We could not be certain either way but manned our stations regardless although no order had been given.

The captain remained in his cabin poring over charts. We knew then that cloud had filled the sails, that the horizon had advanced upon us before we knew it, the deck still firm as any foundation beneath our feet, lifting slightly against the cross-winds that carried a sound open to interpretation. A low vibration diminished and faded soon as we felt it. No one could be sure anything had occurred.

There was neither a sense of impending danger nor anticipation only uncertainty. Each man stranded on the leeward side of thought. Each poised at the threshold of his shipmate's imaginings that verged upon revelation but this diminished also. Such was the unknown latitude of our arrested state and collective awareness. The one thing we suspected and later agreed upon was that all shared in this, unknowingly. Some lustrous cloud expanded above the rigging but just as quickly dissipated and was gone. Later, we tried to shrug this off and make light of it. The sea up to its old tricks again, confabulating stories. Even in daylight when the impossible only made its presence felt at night.

BANISHMENT

Compression of car tyres over wet cobblestones at 3AM. Otherwise, dead silence. One street lamplight bore witness. Two car doors cushioned shut. Then the splintering of wood, flashlights, the barking of orders, a scuffle and muffled cries. A cuffed, hooded figure dragged to the waiting 4WD, its engine thrumming. Acceleration. Once more silence descended as the night held its breath.

The poet stood in the dock. The dark suit given him appeared to be an ill-fit much in the manner of a clown. His head shaven yet clumps of hair remained. His expression stoic. One eye squinted intermittently; a bruise encircled it. Clearly, they had made some attempt to confine his vision. This gave him a discernibly startled look. The charges levelled against him were subversion, challenging the literary status quo. Non-compliance. His refusal to accept the terms of his contract invited ostracism and public ridicule.

Fear, that is, vaporised anger seeped through the hierarchical ranks of the literary establishment. The encrypted sentence dispatched from the Tribunal of Heretical Investigation instructed the provincial branches through the Federation of Subscribed Sycophants to deny him any access to official publishing houses within the state, ad infinitum. Banishment. An exile in his own land. But this was nothing new to him except that now it was passed into law.

It was observed during his mock trial that he was distracted though the accusations made against him demanded no response. Nevertheless, he seemed somewhat absent from the proceedings, and if his lips moved, he said nothing. His gaze fixed upon the ornate, wooden coat of arms on the panelling above the bench where his interlocutors sat staring down at him. But he did not see them. His eyes locked on that escutcheon of authority.

A snake coiled around a sword over a daisy chain of laughing children encircling the handle. A beam of yellow light emanating from the head of the snake like a death ray cut a trench around the children at the haft of the blade entrapping them, yet they were oblivious to this in their gay laughter. It was only years later that the samizdat surfaced. A memoir titled: *The Snake Trench and The Children*. A lament for innocence defiled in the womb. There were reported sightings, but nothing confirmed. The poet had long since vanished.

VISITANT

*'It's not just Einstein's universe, it's ours too.
Our crib and our crypt.'*—Dennis Overbye / The New York Times

The way perception works its way through spaces, those anticipated, unexpected arrivals. Trust in the acrobatic leap and balance beyond the puppet show of mind. Something recalled but never known through the wormhole of the moment. The curvature of vision captured become multiverse, and you the visitant. Faith, too, in the holding pattern and the focus. Just after dusk when shadows reach out, I will light a candle to greet the night, as time momentarily slows, turns briefly to silence, when thought subsides into darkness as prayer. The ghostly prophet declares, 'Is history a record of the deceased?' Not a question to be troubled by. Especially for the living. Death is merely anonymity. O to escape the confines of ordinariness. 'Habit, habit clogs them dumb'. Speech mutates and fails, all else subsides to shadow. 'Wanted: Dead or Alive' trumpets the apotropaic archangel from the lakebed of deepest sleep.

VIEWING PLATFORM

for Bob Orr

Once serried ranks, weathered tree stumps,
silvery as parade helmets off Orini Road.
A few rain lakes swamping low-lying paddocks
not yet dried out by the approaching summer;
hills rising behind in shadow and bush.
Beyond the quarry, Pukemokemoke Reserve;
parking area and squat bridge, the stream
sluggish, rust coloured, weighty in its groove.
You climb a rootbound track up to the summit;
a pole built, elevated viewing platform.
The wide sweep across Orini Downs, and way
off into the distance, Te Aroha, and further,
the Maungakawa Reserve, blurred peaks.
You turn back down through the flickering
compositions of shadowy, filtered light to
the gravel turnaround and wide footbridge.
Not another soul in sight, your car parked there,
frozen in the swing for the return journey.
A bow wave of paddocks, then Tenfoot Road
arrow straight across flatlands, car bonnet
butting cloud over hooped, corrugated iron sheds
under multi-angled, tree stacked windbreaks.
The city glibly emerges beyond the grey
smear of newly moulded subdivision grids—
dusk will soon blur the graph of its outline.
The bells of St. Peter's Cathedral tremulously
shuffle muffled chimes out along the river,
while a handful of birds are silently flung west.

SHALLOW CREEK

His soul got mangled between the
microphone and radio groupies—so what he
breathed, was 'dead air'.

This was way before he slid down
                    a gentle incline, feet first, into
a shallow creek, late at night, drunk.

                Only not to wake up
the next morning, dead—hypothermia, reported
the coroner.

Still, he managed to keep his head above
water, which was more than he managed in life.

                  But this was merely a runnel
of water, suburban, weed infested, poor excuse
for a creek.

He had taken to walking the streets,
a knapsack slung over his shoulder, usually half
pissed, occasionally engaging with

pavement life, like the ladies standing vigil
outside the abortion clinic on Dominion Road.

He joined them in prayer, a rest stop,
                then went on his way to nowhere.

Most things he'd lost, a property, escaped
an early marriage, leaving two kids in his wake,
a history of being bitch-slapped by a
manipulative wife.

Got fired from his last job, as morning DJ
on a ratty radio station; but everyone got fired
from those jobs.

Self-respect, like his ratings, dropped;
what was left for him but to blame family for his
failures, the youngest brother, first to go.

Always the victim to that sort of blonde
chick on the make, or wanting to breed; so he
got used, and then used up, never learnt
                  to stand his ground.

He became someone else, baptised in vodka,
a sinister, inner self emerged, that nurtured
                  dark hatreds, jealousies, melancholia.

I don't think about him much these days,
because who he was had ceased to exist some time
before he died.

                The autopsy report recorded
a few hairline fractures on his skull, from where
he often fell over drunk,
                  just like his father did.

FACTORY TOWN

    The suburb goes one way,
chimney smoke the other. One plane tree; its bole wide as
a well, lava flow of roots massing at the base,
next to the rusty rail line. A derelict munitions factory,
wall graffiti that reads, 'No certainties in this life'.

    Everything seems to be pushing away
from itself—clouds scroll Spanish like a rubric of skunks
on the move, clustering, only to expand and contract.

    Those brick facades
down main street, faded dull as dried blood, each with
its fugitive dank doorway, reeking of urine, or something worse.
There's no one to be seen, maybe the rapture had hit,
but this one orchestrated by neoliberalism.

    Nobody talks about the mayor's
speech he gave a few years back; the brouhaha it caused,
the boosterism, hand claps and backslaps—
turning the munitions factory into a 'museum/theme park,'
'revitalization of our abandoned factory town.'

    Someone talked about making a
documentary, but that never got done. Winter snows make
up for lack of heart, turning this place into some sort
of soft lens crime scene—from the helicopter's perspective,

seems peaceful enough down there, fairyland graveyard,
nicely packaged rust belt town. Trenchant as a death notice.

WHISTLING

Most people's lives turn on a clunky plot, get cosy around
computers, some nice scenery, the muffled comfort we
have come to expect of the everyday; we think nothing of it.

           Do you recall how,
decades earlier, somewhere back in your childhood,
people whistled often and freely, you never really thought
anything of it way back then.

                Something faux friendly or mock-happy
at best. But these days, nobody dares whistle, as though such an
activity had been banned by public decree, or that
fashion, and the age you live in, are against it. That to hear
someone, solitary, whistling, somehow sounds forced, designed
to hide sinister intent.

            A ruse to disguise some terrible act
about to be perpetrated or obsessed over, and that whistling
down a laneway in the dark edgily suggests that airy
pitch has been extracted from a police or ambulance siren,
wrenched loose, stripped away from, stretched out
                into a thin stiletto blade.

You know then that this unseen, breathing entity can
never be trusted, must be avoided at all costs, because this is not
how you remember it, whenever that was—or where.

LAST WORDS

I.M. for John Macnamara

And, finally, gravity brought him low,
for that is nothing other than the inhaling of death.
'I am no better than the best,' exhaled
the poet—and then, unceremoniously, he died.

Ghostly caretaker, he moves amongst his
abstract sculptures of iron and wood,
(an axe frozen onto a painted tree stump) weaving
his labyrinth of dream as quickly discarded

as found, a barely audible breeze through one
hanging mobile, tracking, and slowly abandoning
one painful dream after another—it is,
as always, a triumph of utter dissatisfaction.

THE ARTIFICIAL FLOWER

I suppose one could say, she was surrounded
by a moat of admirers—the Polish beauty, alone
at her table in the Palais Kinsky, in Vienna,
May 1979. Her manner, languid, auburn haired,
it was her woollen dress drew me, large rectangles
chestnut in colour, like a fishing net, wide
as windows—was she naked, otherwise, through
those vacant squares; was this something contrived,
an illusion designed to ensnare? I can't recall.
A large flower head made up of some shiny fabric,
slightly brighter, it seemed, than her woollen
dress of loose rectangles, but part of it, blossomed
lavishly about her hips. She mesmerized me,
she and her dress, auburn hair, that artificial flower
in full, fabric bloom. I took the rose from the
small vase on my table, and walked across the
no-man's-land to where she sat, and presented her
with it, clumsily, I expect—unsurprised, she
turned her full gaze upon me, and what I felt was
paralysis; or maybe I appeared merely gauche,
unsophisticated to her, that is how it seemed.
I can't remember what was exchanged in the salon
at Palais Kinsky that night. A decadent party swam
about her. Someone plucked a champagne flute
from the waiter's platter, threw it back, then with a
bored, dismissive gesture, dropped it onto the
parquet floor with a satisfying smash, quite unaware
that he had done so, or had immediately lost
interest. No one else noticed. The Polish beauty
was already a closed chapter—perhaps she had been
absorbed into the frescoes on the high ceiling,
or become part of the Baroque clutter of the 17th
Century architecture? Wherever she went, she was
no doubt fully at ease, Countess of the Languid
Moment, such as her aristocratic forebears had
practiced and perfected centuries before, those who
still presided at the back of her mind in elegant
counterpoint. I was enthralled by her gaze,

captured by her insouciance, yet dared not cast one
glance toward that metallic, iridescent flower
that lay there, loosely burgeoning upon her thighs.

March 21, 2018

PERIPLUS

What cinnamon bearer, or frankincense
territory, the aromatics of Southern Arabia,
the island of Topazos—the wash of
sea-glut against the hull. Coast always within
sight, toward an undiscovered river mouth
as yet unnamed. Empty ocean beyond.
Shorelines upon which to construct a temple
to those gods left behind. Trading posts
that became future city states, before the time
of flags, awaited them—these mariners
and mapmakers who came to measure a wave,
its sketchy line along an unknown shore.
Far-flung minds, deep curiosity, that overruled
superstition and drove these men into the
strange and unfamiliar; until lost. It was not
fear that made them turn back—periplus;
then to return with a map of coastlines, vibrant
as a lightning strike across the bow at night.

THE OTHER SIDE

After Edward Thomas

"Storm done it, wasn't there last week."
That root system, tortured hieroglyphs, sooty
black as a launching pad after the lift off.

A thick trunk pine tree upended, slumped
riverside, failed launch, collapsed scaffolding,
destined never to make it, recently toppled.

Nearby, sheer drop to the Waikato hauling
light at the turn, in eddies and lassos,
outflanked by that band of totara skirting

this bend in the river. "Peacocke farm."
He gestured toward. "Own a lot of property
hereabouts." Nestled there on the bank.

The road builders with their ring road
haven't extended quite this far or beyond yet.
"Three years off, the bridge, the walkway."

One light, grey-leafed tree turned blue
the other side, foreground, by the farm gate.
Tussock grass knoll, while lower, giving

onto shadowy damp green—a few sheep.
Then the river, light long shifted downstream,
in an act of remembrance, lagging behind.

THE LITERALIST

'Literalists are a bane. Useless, in my experience, to argue with a literalist. I consider literalism to be a perceptual or developmental disability.'—Roger Boyce

His boots were hobnailed with facts and figures, burnished with historical detritus. A man devoid of empathy, a quality which would have interfered with the torrent of commentary and critique governed by a barely disguised self-loathing. A brazen beaver at work building his dam. Such was this self-proclaimed critic, posturing from his virtual lectern in a blog of bombast.

A literary sociopath crouched behind the façade. The clatter of the self-aggrandizing man. He assumed the combative stance of polymath; a Johnsonian behemoth. Refined sensibility was anathema to him, and subtlety he failed to recognize—a dislocation that registered blankly in his mind. Humility was a promise denied him in childhood. He became the schoolyard skulk, surly lipped, and calculated his revenge; all the while that inner voice as leaden echo, 'Notice me! Notice me!'

The years wore on, book critiques accumulated as condescending opinion pieces. Divine afflatus and the ascendancy of poetry remained a persistent mystery, a conundrum that he failed to resolve. The concept was alien to him. Poetry by his reckoning was little more than a mockery of shadow behind rain-blurred windows. Movie reviews were about as close as he ever got to beautiful women.

VIVE LA SANS-DENTS

We broke up cobblestones, just as our forefathers had done, we the 'sans-dents' poor from the sticks, the 'great unwashed.' By the Arc de Triomphe we gathered, stood shoulder-to-shoulder with the 'gilets jaunes' (yellow vests) contingent; were fired upon with tear gas canisters, blasted with water cannon.

At the Champs-Elysées we faced off against police in their black riot gear, shields and rubber batons. For three days fought pitched battles, torched buildings, overturned cars. Some of us fell when we broke through the line, only to advance, and be repelled once more.

An exercise in attraction and repulsion, denial and acceptance, embrace and rejection. One body at war with itself, banners and clarion calls, alarums and flame, our bodies barricading one against the other as lovers do caught in the death struggle between love and hate, until exhaustion resolved the engagement.

Ancient battle cries that arose in the collective mind could barely be distinguished from our ferocious breathing—controlled these limbs in some grotesque pantomime. What we enacted would be preserved in memory, that dark hallway down through which time presses, relentlessly.

We observed the bridge between the wealthy and destitute slowly, inevitably collapse, the rich rose on one side of the chasm and the poor, the 'sans-dents' withdrew on the other. The day of conflagration had come, unavoidable and predestined. Each of those pieces of busted cobblestone we hurled in fury served as ostracon, and the casting of our vote.

THE MIGRATION

Weighty, full moon hoisting over ridge lines.
The flickering of torchlight, isolate, and forked lightning's
flared clematis, but this spelt primeval memory.

These revelations with us still, active,
though our minds have grown to eclipse them; slow
exchange from light into dark that birthed cave art.

                Reflection, momentarily, as torches
flickered through granular caverns; hush of charcoal passing
from fingertips—exhilaration yielding to song under
the moon as memory base.

                We saw death when light fell young,
spilling out over earth's threshold, that it was to our liking—
we tested fear to its limit, reproduced on a killing spree.

We were alive though shadowed by death,
this dissolved into a diminishing dream, half-remembered;
                the haunting of the self.

                Sunset, an anvil aglow in steady retreat,
rays fanning out, off cloud ridges making of them snow caps
but molten. An intensity of silence. Stars missile bright
coming in hard while the blurred negative of our Neolithic
selves materialized.

Every campfire a burning city, but that came later,
we trudged on, seeking difference. Forgiveness lay aeons
ahead. Yet none of us to blame, such a thing

could not exist—we felt no need to forgive ourselves.
The strong and the weak fell equally.
                      Throughout the migrations,
thunder ruminated amongst ravines, along mountain passes.

We met with 'the twang of the arrow, the snap of the bow.'
Our desires were for turmoil, not resolution. An eclipsed age.
                Later, under full sail off the horizon,

either vortex or sextant decided our latitudes, shaped perspective.
Lampblack the sky shot through with star spittle;
                Bronze Age before us meant the game was up.

Our demons shackled there where we wanted them—off
the bowsprit, nodding to the rise and fall of each foreign wave.

We were the blessed, the genesis, or so we thought,
though not the first, humanity came later. Others had arrived by
other routes—guided by the slow burning

                of a collective mind, that glimmered
steadily before them, the gods' breath filling those sails,
chasing the wind—at least, how we recalled it;
we quelled ignorance, claimed everything that lay before us.

When first our hulls scraped beach gravel and sand
violence became a necessary act. Retribution soon followed,
and time began—then exhilaration gave way to fear.

                Increasingly, barbarism met with barbarism,
we clave to the land, eventually outbuilt them, the shadow people.
'Your gods have forsaken you', we cried, 'your ancestors fled.'

                Slate blue to the east, light blown to a ghost cone
out west. Half-moon scything across the valley. We tracked
estuary beyond salt marshes, pushed further inland until we reached

some rocky gorge and rested, built a cairn out of river boulder.
By that simple act—anchored ourselves to the territory,
            the memory of this uncertain place.

Forest darkly folded over hilltops before and behind.
Wind lifted off river surface, elbowed through leafy branches;
birdsong, almost human in its strangeness, startled the men.

All around us that repetitive sense—presence retreating,
nostalgia for something continuously dissolving, irretrievable.

We lived in a time before boundaries confounded us.
Our minds belonged to the moment, endless. Anger we transmuted
into gods and birthed them, eternally castigated for this act.

            Our lives caught between gravity and light
mirrored in conflict. Eden, the betrayal, served as apology by which
we conquered new worlds, over and over again.

After the expulsion, memory dulled, love an illusion born
of despair until finally, we found ourselves alone, upright and braced,
the long winter had begun, that loss, a forgotten treasure.

We defended ourselves against each other through our children
but to no avail. Rubble strewn memory angled into shadow and light,
            made of itself a rose window.

Oak tree leaf, rusted haft of a Templar sword. Clouds laid out flat
as flagstones along the horizon. Bonfires arose to become cathedrals,
            and footfalls sounded cataclysmic.

ANALYTICS

You ask yourself, how much of any real thing is retained?
A question that comes late in life; the first touch, for instance,
but you had forgotten her name, the lingering kiss, how it

merged with others in a seamless continuum though led
to nothing. You remember her broad smile, and the fact that
she was rather lax on dental care, brownish food debris

wedged between the palings of her yellowing teeth that
in recollection, suggested an image of a mud-caulked log
partition, one physical aspect of her you can recall.

Much is overlaid, casually forgotten. There was a paddock,
the days were mellow, it was last of the school holidays.
Brains function to retain but wilfully forget. Remember the

first book you read. Thoughts are a flock of autumnal leaves.
Scientists have found how to activate cells in pig brains
retrieved from an abattoir, kick start synapses, placed within

specially designed tanks, floating there, the neurons pulsing.
These are no animated brains, nothing can be dredged of dreams
to indicate the flare of consciousness (and what passes for

thought), only cellular activity, lost echoes—the long jump
to immortality that banishes death or resurrects the dead belongs
to the province of mythmaking, the circuitry of invention.

Did I imagine I loved you? Too long ago, each loss a dying,
other distractions soon replaced the ache, tremulous expectations
of a revelatory moment, but this usually came later, the faint,

barely audible click of memory's signal, slowly retreating,
could easily have belonged to someone else. Though possibly you
overheard it elsewhere, that it was never yours in the first place.

Maybe it's your brain floating in a chemically, nutrient-rich
solution, every twitch and shudder monitored for signs of cognition,
none of which you are aware of (being dead), what is recorded

beyond the darkening horizon, analytics, logging the swirls,
random currents of the brain's reflexes dissolving into distances—
forever untranslatable, as a moon glazed roof early autumn.

Easter Friday, 2019

CHERT

Wolf howl of the chainsaw, intermittently,
river trending northwest to debouch at Port Waikato.
Cloud fashioned chert tool, another, spearhead
shaped. Buried light, deep shadow, blue dome intact.
Afternoon, winter encroaches, light glissades off
pittosporum demarcating the boundary line.

                Smoky light on paleo cave art,
her hair aglow, coppery as pine needles, there by
the river trail. Leafless, skeleton trees tilt riverward,
give onto Melville that claims the higher ground.
Backyard shed windows boarded up with plywood;
a broody suburb, predominately state houses.
Battle standards flag the sky, gradually, day bleeds
out into sunset. Traffic clots Cobham Drive.

Meanwhile, down by the river between bridges
and piers, hanging gardens—mapping coordinates.
Currents skirt an islet, angled afternoon light,
an electrum shudder expands, dims downstream.
Beneath the slide rule of traffic, rowing fours,
dragonflies under Victoria Bridge's iron shadow.

LADY OF THE MURALS

'The memory of you keeps calling after me like a rolling train.'—Bob Dylan & Sam Shepard / Brownsville Girl

'Out of a headstrong cloud column emerged one square-rigged ship, buckled to the waves ...' But here the story neither begins nor ends. "The entire landscape, graveyard, public gardens, Peacocke farmstead over the river, extensively undermined by rabbits," you answered in response to her query about the innumerable burrows, and promptly imagined the whole shebang catacombed with intersections and way stations, a veritable metro-subway system stretching for leagues—Kingdom of the Rabbit.

That smile O how it illuminated her calm, Byzantine beauty. Lady of the Murals. This Russian student, newly arrived to complete her Masters in Mesmerisation. You talked easily for an hour or so then parted. She pointed out that her name, Katerina, had Greek origins, "like the Orthodox Church," she explained. Looking back, across to that trig station in the afternoon light, you observed within its framework a broad, tree-lined boulevard. Dusk, and headlights shimmering off into some other century, already dissolved in space-time, seemingly vanished through the wormhole.

Before walking away you had already taken those farewell steps in your mind, embraced all you perceived of her in that sustained, shared moment. Departure can be understood as symbolic acknowledgement, an inverted greeting yet barely sensed, become footnote to this manufactured recollection. A brief encounter. Beneath the congealed sunset you tracked back to your car, strategically positioned for an unhurried exit, parked there amongst the memorial plaques and headstones.

STAMP MILL

"If that's what it is—we're bleeped!" stated the anchorwoman across the wetlands of CNN. Tweets as bubbles breaking the surface of an aquarium, soft plosives, then nothing. The stopes and drifts of investigative reporting hammered home with stamp mill authority. Visual recognition of white noise. In the other camp, *vox populi*, rigged interviews favoured by the right-wing networks preaching to the blue-collar workers laid off from factories and coal mines, passed over by legislators, while the stringer sounds off on 'Make America Great Again'. He and his crew, wing men to the West Wing, every man jack of them. From desert to red mud country. Once more the world distorts in a hall of mirrors, and denial stunt doubles for truth. But you are here, removed from the clamour. A flotilla of black swans riding at anchor on Lake Karapiro (though more loch than lake) with its drowned village like something out of a J.G. Ballard novel. A handful of bunker and barn style homesteads passed on the way to 'Little Waipa Reserve' turn off. This stretch of lake a quiet backwater, magpies amidst a carillon of pine on the far side. The clear, triple call of California quail, first heard filtering out of the desert in *The High Chaparral* TV series late '60s. Toi toi flares up, bright signal stations. You head back into the city. The day subsides west, cirrus cloud laid out crumpled as tinfoil. Meanwhile, the flat-topped River Explorer, resembling a floating fairground tent, drums upstream on its daily round through peat country to The Narrows.

OTHERWISE

She inhabited that shut down, roller door look. *Clang!* Head slightly bowed, looked neither left nor right, stared obliquely ahead. Her mouth, set like a concrete curb. You caught a passing glimpse as you turned on the roundabout. A stranger going about her daily chores. You thought nothing about it at the time. Maybe she dreamed a life in some Lego Cube house built to resemble a half-opened chest of drawers, opening out onto river views in chain mail light. Supposedly happy in an illusory sort of way but then, to observe is not to judge, so who can say? We take our chances at whatever cost though hardly any of this cause for concern.

In the Land of Otherwise, beware the manipulative hipster *qua* careerist, one who has mastered the art of upfront subterfuge. 'Tis a cove one would not pull into willingly. Unless forced by some barometric pressure drop in the Cycladic trope of the compartmentalized mind. Entirely against one's will no doubt, if indeed such a thing were possible. O wind of ill-intent. Plug your ears with beeswax, lash yourself to the masthead. Pass by traveller, this is no country for old men nor any man. Such hollow, academic dissembling by echolocation may track you down yet. Nothing's lost so what's left to discover? Let such distortions muffle to silence in your wake, Caravaggio of the Industrial *noir* poetic. Success means fulfilling some other need. Gods don't play favourites, all is equidistant. Real life swarms elsewhere.

THE BRASHER DOUBLOON (1947)

Just another day of dames slamming doors. Downtown L.A. Bunker Hill. Once a choice place to live, now a place for those with no choice. Fire traps and dirty tenements. He'd hard-questioned the rare coin dealer who didn't know his time was up. The Western Union Telegram waiting for him back at his Hollywood office bluntly stated, 'Services no longer required.'

The wealthy family who hired him to find the stolen Brasher Doubloon lay behind the theft, blackmail and homicides. The body count mounted daily and barely a week on the job. The client's secretary, deranged, terrified of the matriarch, had already fallen for Marlowe and his snap brim trilby. She held the answers as he held her. The temperature dropped before the rain did, then warmed again.

Harbourside city and shot put weather. The living are memories of the dead and dream is the four-poster bed of *Ars Poetica*. Call it by its real name. *The Takedown*. 'O the poverty of the boulevards!' slams in right on cue. Pick any slide show and add your favourite festival. Feels like waiting for either sermon or summons.

The day leaned back like some Robert Mitchum swagger. Any hedge is a maze in waiting, he reasoned. No leads, nothing you could poke a night stick at anyways. A lowering, crumpled tarp of cloud darkened. One slate slab on a blue backdrop. He recalled how Mulholland Dam's curve reminded him of an eyeball though with lopsided, monocular vision. Spillway leaky as a tear duct running from it. He saw the occluded shape at distance in sharp focus under pressure.

SIREN CITY

           Skid mark sunset. Twilight.
Cleft leaf harbours shadow memory. The first porchlight star,
Venus kicks in. The world swings wide in his mind,
a sounding board of particled concentration.

           Loneliness, for him
an instinct. Otherwise, all that rebounds is the broken
compass of his anger, displaced, his thoughts untethered.

           English, then Mandarin, assault the caregiver.
An emphatic, pump-action delivery interspersed
with 'Apple', 'Bill Gates' (a favourite), 'Jobs', 'Taylor
Swift', the domain over which he alone rules, erratically
and loud.

           I am part of this, Siren City resident,
a close-by neighbour, and here within this zone, at ground
zero, subjected to these disruptions. Dumping ground
for the psychiatrically displaced.

           Meanwhile, the hospital
gleams on the horizon, white as a luxury liner, west of here.

DON'T BE ALARMED

Banksy on his balcony at The Walled Off
Hotel imploding the barrier a leap away,
watchtowers left and right. The Israeli land
grab barricade winding off out of sight;
they play it systematic, and with stealth.
He sees it otherwise, maps his grid, memory
coordinates, seals up busted holes with
plaster to stop the darkness seeping through.

Silence before the rumour. A carriage
of thunder rolled away, cannon fire heard
in a cloud bank. Then the recoil, as
everything slipped back into place, millennia
hence. Don't be alarmed. Whatever befalls,
you are pitched, once again, into the chasm.
The millennial shuffle. Ploughshare moon
on a lopsided sky. Let the church bells toll
sublime from the primal arsenal.

Antediluvian breath, the twelve tribes
seeking the unattainable. Not your typical,
postmenopausal suburban scene, saved by the
flowerpot and watering can. The bullet hole
he paints on concrete glistens bright as crystal,
'The Scar of Bethlehem', over Palestine, too.
A woman heard at distance undeniably
emphatic, even in warbled laughter—
and poetry the articulation of forgetfulness.

STEPS

Bookshelves are cityscapes, steps in any given
library, your hand on the pulse, regard this simply as
benediction that did not prove false, slightly abrasive
underhand (the) hand, resting momentarily.

       Is this the definition of
loneliness, itself merely sentiment stretching into
indulgence? As with any reflection, you do not wish
to overstay your welcome—an echo returning unto
itself, oblations to absent gods eternally present.

       Shake the carpet of memory;
the first thing seen arriving in LA (a brief stay),
though sexy Venice Beach beckoned, before taking
a bus to San Francisco, was the American flag
fluttering atop a building (any building) and two cops
with carbines casually standing guard on the steps
outside the foyer, a thin trail of blood leading to it.
Real as a movie set. Welcome to America!

       You soon realized that sex
is the dream (one of them), strolling hand-in-hand
with violence down the boulevard, one step up
into heightened awareness. An everyday occurrence,
the constant, collective consciousness that
washed over you, stepping into the slipstream;
thankfully, absorbed by the anonymity of cityscape.

GO THE DISTANCE

An elderly lady, wearing shades and head scarf, midwinter, in a bus shelter, looking like a torn down poster, pressed into the corner. Illusory vigilance as you stare once again into the chasm. Look up. Behold the original blueprint unrolled there. A tableau that far exceeds the comet's million-mile tail. Trick or treat, we overburden the balancing scales, upset the apple cart. Go count the spiral galaxies contained within tree rings.

Women's Thai Kick Boxing World Welterweight, elbow jolt, fisticuffs, challenge. The Australian commentator states, "Her face is a horror show." And later, "Her nose is a Picasso." End of round three and the best of five. The Dutch champ chick ahead on points. Skilled in reverse kick to kidneys, knee drop, elbow smash. They go the distance. "Her face (pause) looks like someone's set it on fire and put it out with an axe," proclaims the Australian. His American co-host quips deadpan, "That's very descriptive." Life thumps on. Go count the light years on your déjà vu return orbit.

Here comes the clattering horse drawn caravan, its canvas sides flapping the Last Supper in crude detail, Christ and his apostles jostling in swallowing folds as the travelling players pass through. The whole scene animated in great gulping waves down a tunnel sized gullet. O waste and aridity of deserts! Ghostly footage heading out from cerebellum country. What remains, uncharted territory before the inevitable leap, our faith fallen flat, or by some other leap made, regardless?

THE COMMON GOOD

Reassurances are little more than well-meant falsehoods. 'I do not apologize for the war and subsequent genocide. I did my duty,' wrote the general in his unpublished memoir, marked: EMBARGOED: 50 YEARS. Combat medals and citations testament to his fealty. He had served his country with unfaltering distinction, fiercely defended its corporate, global interests.

The general wanted to be remembered as the bright star who rode high in the saddle. *Inter-Generational Conflict. Mutual Destruction. The End Game.* These represented key chapter headings under the section marked 'Trade Craft'. A tribe is defined by those who oppose it. He argued that this should be strategically interpreted as meaning the military under his command did not condone ownership in the traditional, cultural sense of first nation peoples, but did with impunity lay claim to another's territory in the interests of The Common Good. Non-Negotiable. "History, right there!" he said.

The expediency of a pre-emptive, surgical strike negated calls for restraint or any subordinate opposition to massacre. "Women and children first. Spare no one," joked the General in the company of fellow officers. He scrawled across the 'manifesto-cum-memoir' THE END JUSTIFIES THE MEANS. He is Everyman. Axis mundi. Earthbound Colossus and Empire Builder. Dream of the Rood. Tree/Cross Incarnate. Redemption and torture. Equalizer in the devil's DNA. Already become monument without a tomb.

BIG DATA

White marble. The mountains of Luni. Is the creative act once realized an escape from Self? The pyramidal sea, for instance, wedged firmly in the hill cleft. Burnished. Moon and stars—stairway that fans out into the marble world of Michelangelo. His sanctuary, those mountains. A stage upon which to strut one's stuff. Beseeching dark matter to show itself, waiting for the answer that never comes which, by countless astronomical units, has not reached us yet beyond the Platonic Absolute, the gravelly ring systems of gas giants, over the Blakean convulsions of Jupiter, older than the Big Bang, calibrated by the latest elliptical hula hoop simulations, to give the ghost a skeleton. Does memory of all things exist independently of mind?

We retreat inevitably into the mental bomb shelters of expediency. 21st Century cloud banquet retrieves the moment. One Tudor style apartment block newly completed. Ethnicities: subcontinent. Employment: computer programmers and/or gamers. God is dead replaced by Big Data. A driveway bullet-straight leads back from it. Neighbourhood: occasional low life with the eyes of dugongs. Conventional, middle-of-the-road, inner suburbia. A quadraphonic dog barked, chased its DNA, then vanished. Another sunset. This one with deserts flaring in its wake—over storage tanks at Port Jaffa breakwater. Through the *Portara* (Great Door) to the unfinished Temple of Apollo, overlooking the sea on Naxos. Dreams, too, of a worked-out marble quarry, and the sculptor within the enfolding light remembered there.

WAY OF LIFE

The Medusa head burst from Taal volcano,
Luzon Island, crackling with lightning
and godly invective, fourteen miles out from
Manila, as if some giant steam engine
thundered by under the mantle billowing ash
and smoke on track along the Pacific Rim
of Fire.

      American dream, the shredded
coat of David. So much for multiplicity.
"Used to be if you were a hard luck kid in
a dead-end town in a fly over state you learned
to play guitar or drums." "At least along the
way something instead of nothing." Elizabeth
Wurtzel reads from her book, *Creatocracy*
at the Strand. "Lament for a way of life that's
lost, for all that will no longer be," swings
through the carnage of American pop culture.
"Money explains everything."

"The Eagles sound like cocaine going
up someone's nose." She pauses, sips from
bottled water. "Money is where the action
is." "The teenager is gone, the lineal link
between childhood and responsibility."
"Gone, just like the record album," she says,
"love requires serious moonlight."

      "We are here to be entertained
and not do a google search." Lizzie reads,
"we are here to have fun." Speeds through the
wreckage, hoping to outrun the black dog
of depression, addiction, suicidal love.
The lamp of hope swings way in the distance,
beyond and unattainable. False hope lies
within easy reach. Elizabeth Wurtzel. I.M.

SCAFFOLDING

Scaffolding fixed onto the sky firm as
teeth braces, is flooded by it. Empty cathedral
of air housing some ruin or dwelling under
construction that will one day become before
a different sky—new scaffolding.

          Hear the years tighten
their bolts and creak, while another body drops,
rigid as a pole. The years pass blindly by,
hit the ground of remembrance. There was a war,
and then another, where most who lived it
were forgotten, or wished that they had been.

Crimes are the best kept secrets; this is
written into the constitution of the heart, hidden
under scaffolding of bone, where we build
and rebuild, just as we dismantle with each breath,
taken and released. Each life a lesson learned
or lost. Scaffolding sharp as any crucifixion set
upon the skyline.

          Superman, in profile,
middle distance, flying across the cityscape,
his cape tremulous, aflutter—seen through an
open window, caught in a balletic stance, head
turned elegantly toward the camera, an apartment
block balanced with one hand, a gigantic platter,
whisked away to safety.

TO WHAT?

You can't beat death, no way, death
is the finishing line, and life the shadow cast
over that retreating horizon.

        So, what to do? You can't.
They say the universe is expanding, but don't
know why—to what?

And what is infinity anyhow, questions
are not answers, though probably as close as
we can ever get—to what? Questioning.

        I have my own theory
that astrophysicists would guffaw at. Yes,
the universe is expanding, continuously, into
nothingness—

        it is the migration, fountain-
head, ever expanding flock of souls departing
this planet, flooding the cosmos.

That great deluge of souls, into the
grand, speculative covenant of nothingness,
that is endless, multidirectional, broad

as any godly smile, lighting up the dark,
chasing infinity, to remember what has been
lost. Forever.

        That is why the universe
is expanding—diffusion of collective memory.
It is circular.

DISTANT

"A mass of brass /
That sea looks, blazing underneath!"
—Robert Browning: *Le Byron De Nos Jours*

Bartender at the Pirate Bar, Hydra, moved
rhythmically to the 'Sultans Of Swing' nightly.
"His song," you said, Greek girl from Alexandria,
the first to complicitly use me on that island;
how many others had you also? Your walls blankly
white (estranged artist parents, you told me),
were your eyes blank, too, or simply resigned?

I returned to that bar, offended, berated you
who listened sadly, said nothing, took me to your
bed a second time back in 1979. O stranger still,
your distant anonymity. All of us are tremulously
damaged, only admit to it with yearning bodies,
rarely our hearts. Loneliness, constant lover, patrols
borders of rejection, haunts us yet, down through
the wilderness of years—is that what you felt?

PREFACE TO A FOREST

Even guesswork is inspiration if we trust it,
allow ourselves to balance on the precipice of
momentary belief, the possible, that awaits
as safety net below.

                  Magpies, sharp as blades, move
across pine needles, light turning on its shield.
Did you hear the exaggerated rush of air
through branches? This is the falling, reversed
back to that step before you took it;
preface to a forest. Afterwards, a small breeze
by which leaves played piano keys.

                  For the monk in his cell, play
of shadow upon the mat. See how he embraces
his God, whose arms, flung wide, make
an amphitheatre, and he at the centre of it, lifted
into the acoustic of his prayer. He recalls the
ancient dress code; sacrifice—art before religion,
memory before art. His cell a cave, as candle
flame danced, shadows applauded.

It was then he knew the still point, pushed
by deep silence, the shouldered, coastal hills,
darkening; though, it was the moon's
tabloid that billboarded the waves' ragged
italic, and halted him as he heard.

CRANIAL BUNKER

Companionable, like the moon but not, lonely as neon
that with its fizzing imitates the sound thin rain makes in the
memory, in a greasy diner late at night.

This is more an image mimicking what you recall
that sound made, while neon and footsteps are paired in the
frame extracted from this, the pavement monochrome,
shiny wet.
          So, you ask, 'What are we part of?'

Lack of definition in country or self, is that diminishment too,
something missed out on? Small towns, each with
its own abattoir as anchor.
          But these are shutting down, one by one,

towns cast adrift, while unemployment flaps predatory wings
throughout those forlorn river valleys.

Aflame, the plane fell like a bejewelled crucifix,
or so it seemed, but that was only the sunset. Did the pilot
eject safely? You guessed he landed amongst the

stooks and braided rows of stubble, dragging the cloud of
his parachute behind him, silhouetted as a scarecrow, dancing.
Yet that was only the topdressing plane landing in a

nondescript paddock with no windsock to be seen.
There is no war going on here, at least, not a physical one—
the mind's eye peers out through its cranial bunker.

Small towns are a microcosm of what the world is,
'the good, the bad, and the very ugly,' a quick-change vaudeville
routine where most times you don't hear the whispers,
               just feel them, which likely have you in their

crosshairs, assassinated a hundred times over, secure
you think, behind your shrubby foliage, though
that has become a forgotten age,
               and one you left years ago.

Is what you think of them what they think of you?
Probably. Poisonous as Metaxa, a vile taste on the tongue
come morning, a lingering guilt that you dare not share.

               Sometimes, I go back beyond
self (small comfort), and wonder how I ever fared before
the ambush. When distance fitted the cliché
               'at a safe remove'

but had to tread carefully, something to do with weak ankles,
and unseen, perilous potholes.

FOREST OF STARS

An impossible conveyor belt of zeros dictate the end of the universe—is nothing something? That we should care when humanity is not there; retrograde, an apology at best, the damage done. So we repeat and call it history. A parallel universe from the Big Bang (God's hand clenched to a fist), then released. Heavy elements taking flight, a flock of birds to flood emptiness, making of it a contrast, one of our deepest dreams. Nothing escapes, everything haunts. What is gained is lost. We value what must evaporate, destruction in an eye blink—to see, is to know nothing, and nothing is the uninhabited and unknown. We populate doubt, the reservoir of fear with our dreams like lily pads in bloom upon the lake's surface. Beauteous illusions to remind ourselves that we are alive, that we could capture nothingness, to recreate ourselves, endlessly, in this circular argument of life and death. The mind's expansion into nothingness, lost amongst a forest of stars, fording rapids of light, to create a God that does not exist. To remember that each life knows one stilled moment, in totality—is the eternal equation.

THAT FARTHER SHORE

I.M. Rudi Krausmann / 1933-2019

DEAR RUDI, it was following the moon through cloud, that man invented sailing; all invention is mimicry, memory. I heard of your death a year late, forgive me for not getting back to you sooner. The immigrant is, after all, a Colossus astride two cultures; that of his birth, and that of his death. The stance he takes between these two countries is his balancing, around which the winds of change dance, macabre or otherwise.

I have your book of poems, *'From Another Shore'* (1975) before me inscribed, *'For Stephen from NZ Under'*. Given to me soon after I arrived on that other shore late 1986. I open your book and see this from *'Conquests'*: '*6. Don't waste your language on the dead. On the corpses the / systems bloom. / The imagination is imprisoned by its own festival.*'

When we first met, you challenged me. I laughed, and said, "It's okay Rudi, I have blue eyes." I knew that you had been one of the Hitler Youth. It was what your generation did by decree. An Austrian under the German heel. We became firm friends. You said to me once, "Only take from life what you need." Maybe you were right, though life takes more from us than we request, too. That farther shore you have now reached, granted an eternal visa—home at last.

May 8, 2020

JENES FERNERE UFER

Zum Gedenken an Rudi Krausmann / 1933-2019

LIEBER RUDI, indem er dem Mond durch Wolken folgte, erfand der Mensch das Segeln; jede Erfindung ist Mimikry, Erinnerung. Ich habe von deinem Tod ein Jahr zu spät gehört, verzeih mir, dass ich nicht früher darauf reagiert habe. Der Immigrant ist schließlich ein Koloss, der mit beiden Füßen in verschiedenen Kulturen steht; der seiner Geburt und der seines Todes. Die Stellung zwischen diesen beiden Ländern, die er einnimmt, ist sein Balanceakt, um den die Winde des Wandels tanzen, ob es ein Totentanz ist oder nicht.

Ich habe deinen Gedichtband *'From Another Shore'* (1975) vor mir liegen mit der Widmung *'For Stephen from NZ Under'*. Ein Geschenk für mich, bald nachdem ich an jenem anderen Ufer Ende 1986 angekommen war. Ich öffne dein Buch und sehe dies aus *'Conquests'*: *'6. Don't waste your language on the dead. On the corpses the / systems bloom. / The imagination is imprisoned by its own festival.'*

Als wir uns kennenlernten, hast du mich herausgefordert. Ich lachte und sagte, "Ist schon in Ordnung, Rudi, ich habe blaue Augen". Ich wusste, dass du in der Hitlerjugend gewesen warst. Das war deiner Generation so verordnet. Ein Österreicher unter dem deutschen Stiefelabsatz. Wir wurden enge Freunde. Du hast mir einmal gesagt, "Nimm dir vom Leben nur das, was du brauchst." Vielleicht hattest du recht, obwohl das Leben auch mehr von uns nimmt, als wir verlangen. Jenes fernere Ufer, das du nun erreicht hast, gewährte ein ewiges Visum—endlich zu Hause.

Übersetzung: Heinz. L. Kretzenbacher

THE POLITICIAN

The skin is an external nervous system. However, being thick-skinned, that is, impervious to others, the politician failed to notice this. His skin was his armour. Yet those eyes betrayed him, emanating a sense of self-entitlement which overruled any other consideration subservient to that one singular ambition; self-adulation in an accelerated trajectory toward incontestable power. Isolation, for him, meant utter domination over his minions and detractors.

Sleep remained uninterrupted and dreamless. He traversed his daily ambitions negotiating a minefield, every step a caution that left nothing to chance. The day of the great rally had arrived. The crowd was an engine roar. He pressed his palm to his chest beneath the flag. Was his thought faster than the bullet that shattered his parietal plates; did time slow for one nanosecond to register regret for the lies and prevarication, for the statements he believed were for the greater good; did his brain waves spike in that instant seeking escape from the deadly projectile flatlining toward his termination from all earthly obligations; did that thought faster than light allow him one final breath of forgiveness, and if so, was it summarily rejected?

What remained was a public record of iniquities much as expected. The politician reduced to a footnote in history, denied a commemorative plaque. The empire he sought pooled into a halo of blood and bone fragment about his broken skull, there beneath the podium, in the Rose Garden, as cameras whirred and clicked, as his family scattered like a flock of flushed fowl, as security men swooped and dived, as his body twitched one final salute. An afternoon like any other midsummer, a polished sky, the sun deflected bonfires off glass skyscrapers, turned serpentine in the dark shades of his henchmen.

June 20, 2020

ANTHONY KINGSMILL-LUNN (1926-1993)

with thanks to Ann Diamond, fellow Hydriot

I am old enough now to talk with ghosts—they draw closer. Beyond the scent of thyme, you saw through pretension, painter of the Soho School, took me under your wing. You drank me under the table, one tin cup of Retsina after another on Hydra, refuge for painters and poets, musicians. You invited me back to your villa, fifteen minutes from port along the coast to Kamini, at the top of the gully. Your partner at the time, so much younger, silent mostly, wan, a Pre-Raphaelite beauty, said to me, "Watch this." As she prodded you out of your drunken stupor. How you growled and snapped awake. Maybe a cruel party trick for houseguests, who can say? Brilliant, delicate painter, acrylics and watercolours, a disciple of Cézanne, who captured that silvery light, the glowing whitewashed villas, so long ago. You told me 'grey' was the most elusive colour in nature. Would you have observed that the underside of a leaf is cloud coloured?

And trust, too, where you trusted no one. An original, first edition of your friend the poet, George Barker, inscribed and signed, you lent me to read, which in your absence I returned via Bill's Bar where we often met, prior to my departure. A return to Athens, briefly, then the Magic Bus to Salzburg, thence on to Vienna to fall in love, but that road lay some weeks ahead. Every poem is a letter to the lost and abandoned, those guardians of memory, of pain and loss. Even then, I sensed I would salute you years hence, where your ghost lay in wait. Hydra, those women who would take you, and take you into them, meant a shared moment of nothingness, pleasure for its own sake without meaning. How distant it all seems now—a dream; failed expectations, evaporations. You would have embraced mediaeval science that saw 'vision as light "dwelling" in the eye.' I heard you had died in poverty, a clochard, on the streets of Paris, March 13, 1993. That City of Light where you once studied at the École de Paris, telling tales of your friendship with Leonard Cohen for money and drink—where was your friend then who might have come to your aid, though likely your pride would not have allowed it? Anthony, rest easy in whatever ring of moss that now encircles you. True artist, a man who accepted me on trust alone.

September 18, 2020

FIG TREE

Remembering Christina from Baden-Baden on Hydra

        Nothing seemed significant about it;
but this appeared to me over and over again,
there set in a recess on the hillside off the track
leading up from the harbour cafes and shops on Hydra—
one fig tree, early winter, late November 1979.

        I hold this as memory I carried
with me from an arched, Venetian stone bridge over
some small stream or ravine along the coast,
to where she resided; either coming back, or going
over that ancient bridge, late in the evening, with the
German girl, she clutching a bottle of Demestica,
as she stumbled, nearly tripped—

        who read my mind as I read hers
later into the night. "Now you have everything you
want," she whispered to me.

The hum at the back of the head making of it an
amphitheatre for voices, echoes, oracles. I again recall
that fig tree, standing there by the track, on the
island of Hydra, the memory of my night with her,
yearningly recent, reverberating within me as I passed
the fig tree to where I had stayed amongst
the whitewashed villas high up on that mountainous
island—

        witness to how my senses had
vibrated like the strings of a finely tuned lute at the
back of my head in one stilled, sensual moment,
as I paused and passed on by.

TENT FLAP

A self-parody

'Fish that flex are as birds that fly,' and, 'The flax bush
bloom throws down its gauntlet,' opines the oracle poet.

                    "Roll Up!" "Roll Up!"
cries the spruiker. "Come see the sage in the freak's tent
who glows like a 40w bulb."

"A uterus is an Aladdin's Cave of memory set on repeat,"
he proclaims, flickeringly.

Meanwhile, the cube digging lifts another suburb out of
some paddock, as turned clay lashes out orange.

                      Tea Estate: ZEALONG.
A giant ceramic tea leaf, glazed white, at distance, dead
centre, between the white monumental gate posts.

Parallel poplars lined up shoulder to shoulder,
before the processing plant, preside as guard of honour,
standing upright as apostles.

                      The estate boasts rectitude,
post-colonial style, tea plantings banded down and across
the hill's biceps.

A moth, mate-waltzing its shadow over the ceiling,
                    mirrored bouncing silent as a tent flap.

"If the mind were understood as city, there would be riots in
the streets", and, "We are captain of our own souls,
                    but who commands the life-raft?"

Puddles stretched silkily over the pavement, shadow gnawed
               palings, or light shredded off fence lines.

"Whales beaching re-enact what became Homo sapiens
departing the pre-biotic soup," then, "A species
               is like any relationship, good while it lasts."

               The Ferris Wheel creaks to a halt;
one last, amplified gasp, the sage long gone, the tent flap
slaps back—emptiness, an indrawn breath.

Lights dim, casually cease, slow blink, and then stillness.

EPIGRAMS FOR THE DISENCHANTED

An Informal Survey

1. Folk don't express emotion openly these days because they can't trust themselves.

2. God save me from the hipster trendoids; like a plague of wasps in a beech forest.

3. Normality in true born poets might be considered a state of insanity.

4. Every poem is a letter to the lost and abandoned, those guardians of memory.

5. Minor poets are as carp to ponds—an infestation.

6. Ego beyond its reach validates nothing other than vanity as mime.

7. What is success after all, but the ability to use one's talent, and to lie.

8. The secret of memory is the silent echo, and myth is the reservoir of recall.

9. Dusk: the pride of the blackbird, the privacy of the thrush.

10. Definition of love: couples constantly apologizing to each other.

11. Someone offends. I project them into the burning core of this planet. I recycle.

12. The world is round as a bullet hole—and this galaxy our exit wound.

13. He gripped that bouquet of flowers as he would a can of beer.

14. Every great poem published is a
spell cast. Poetry is sound heard by the mind.

15. The American flag pulsates like a pole
dancer on heat.

16. All religions are founded on paganism;
the engendering of the human spirit.

17. The masses don't want truth. They want
reassurance. Truth to them is isolation.

18. Consider the lilies of the field, and then
regard the cowpats.

19. What is old age, after all, but an apology
for youth.

20. Trace your eye-socket, that tells you how
your skeleton stares absently—in death.

21. A cruel woman gave me a kindly smile /
given I had not been kissed in a while.

22. If you can honestly say a poem you
read arrested time, then you've read a great poem.

23. Earth glows as a coloured globe
in a waste-verse of infinite darkness. Party time.

24. When a woman puts her lights on full
beam to attract a man, it is simply self-defence.

25. I'm suffering from solar system syndrome;
no escape pod.

26. Every failed image for an artist—is an
act of depression, then revelation.

27. The best of poetry dignifies inquiry and
elevates our questioning.

28. We are all victims of mortality, as the years pile up, and tumble into nothingness.

29. The rustic pointed nor'east and nor'west giving directions. He knew his limits.

30. You cannot escape truth; if you try to, it becomes doubt.

31. My relationships with women were failures, but one-night stands were successes.

32. The trick about being dead is to remind those alive your art & belief was worth it.

33. For the word to be heard, it needs silence, hunting ground of the echo.

34. Never take it personally. History is the record of remembered insults.

35. Death does not frighten me. But I am a coward when it comes to mortality.

36. Relentless data bombardment is a stun grenade thrown into the consciousness.

37. The poet as teleologist is the fearless poet who defends truth against falsehood.

38. What is memory but building upon your own accumulative ruins.

39. If dream is the unmade bed of poetry, loneliness is the fear of not being understood.

40. Clear sky. The moon full. A burning silver coin. Rooftops are sheets of ice.

41. The ancients understood mortality as hard reality: ergo; they were visionary.

42. The illusion of what is important is to be caught up in immediacy.

43. Infinity is just another word for nothing; the lie we bestow upon chronology.

44. The errors of the imagination are often articles of great beauty.

45. What else is pole dancing but the erotic re-enactment of the tree of good & evil.

46. Like straddling the Rings of Saturn, throwing stones at each other. A relationship.

47. Dusk. Car doors closing is a neighbourhood —repeated, a police squad.

48. Looking back, he jettisoned her image like so much space junk.

49. He was reincarnated twelve times before he managed to write his own epitaph.

50. Back country road, view over an expansive estuary, and light a mediaeval pageant.

51. "The world is drenched in the winding sheet of lost loves," proclaimed Edith.

52. Starlings are the closest thing we have to Messerschmitts, and myna birds to Nazis.

53. O nothing shallow about her at all, she was an exercise in speleology.

54. Women are by nature naturally generous; especially when they refuse you.

55. The mediaeval mind would contend that Fate is the machinery of Providence.

56. The planet pandemic of overpopulation;
nature kicks back & culls. Suck it in.

57. The concept of one God rather than
an amphitheatre of gods is a corporate invention.

58. Everything that once existed, does—as
shadows are the memory of light.

59. It's all up for grabs. The lines are drawn.
The columns of the temple have fallen.

60. We believe in beauty because it offers us
the illusion of immortality.

61. The appalling question of consciousness
and history as guilt: Homo sapiens/mortality.

62. Looking back, I see my weakness was never
to recognize when I should leave a woman.

63. Where would Magritte be without his
umbrella but himself thinking about it.

64. The greatest art relies upon nuance as an
avenue into memory.

65. The sense of missing something, but what—
is this the same as having lost something?

66. I miss past chapters in my life; not in
and of themselves—but because they are gone.

67. The secret of women's allure is that beauty
supersedes sex.

68. Ghosts within our heads are extrapolations
into reality—projections of paranoia.

69. Poetry is the subtlety of difference. Much
that needs to be left unsaid.

70. When time takes flight it is memory; no sooner seen than forgotten.

71. A dictator can't release his hold on power; it's synonymous with immortality.

72. That look she gave was an eyeblink, some scene in a movie not yet shot.

73. Ink of another's thunder gravitationally held in place; a funeral mask.

74. He felt diminished as a drawbridge operator in a giant aquarium.

75. A poet who thinks aloud and calls it poetry is an undisciplined poet, or not one.

76. To be truly alive? I ride the range, wait for revelation, not heart attack. No God.

77. Too many distractions in the physical world, blame it on gravity.

78. If I am going to be cursed, let it be completely cursed, that way I know where I am.

79. If the universe expands, accelerates into nothingness—can nothing exist?

80. Exact perception, is simplicity of expression, and style a quality of mind.

81. Remember, it's not always a case of manic depression—every day's a new reality.

82. To be caught between chaos and reality is the designation of Limbo.

83. What folk consider fact, is irrevocable; climate change, for example—cannot be denied.

84. Calvinism, self-righteousness, at its most lenient is merely smug paternalism.

85. The BMW comes into view. Camera closes in, close-up—licks the brand belly button.

86. A graduate. That hard work finally paid off! Now one can get a job as a janitor.

87. I do not fall in love—because I could not handle the loss.

88. A fireman might be considered one who edits a rubric event.

89. What is the game of life but a roll of the dice. There is no God only lotto.

90. Living is the ritualistic dance in a futile effort to keep death at bay.

91. Aging feels like a huge responsibility that I am not yet mature enough to cope with.

92. A feeling of relief translates as the sense of freedom from responsibility.

93. The adventure of youth invariably ends in sex—the failure of the Romantic Dream.

94. Endless vistas of youth. The rising foothills of age; thankfully, I am long-sighted.

95. A handful of grain does not a St. Francis make, nor does it placate the wild boar.

96. When all the boundaries break down honesty gives way to madness and freedom.

97. But what is despair, after all, but the letting go of the past.

98. Such is our species, we create
gods to comfort us against mortality. We invent.

99. Life is a board game where death is
one jump ahead of your next move.

100. There is no God. Only frantic imaginings
of Sci Fi. We are the gods.

101. Why the world is in chaos? Given all our
indulgences, we can't believe we will die.

102. Immediacy eradicates visual recall—
thus, Google maps.

103. Jacob's Ladder, the twisted DNA of our
species spiralling back upon itself, growth as memory.

104. "I travel towards the plain of age, through
the mountain-heights of youth," sang the Skald.

105. Stand in any one spot long enough, and
you will observe the subtleties in silence.

106. Vision is compressed thought
where time ceases to exist—the eternal moment.

107. The medium of prophecy is water, and
how light slows river flow.

108. The Beatles are basically Coronation
Street on speed.

109. What is that formless, nagging doubt that
haunts, but the inner child who blames.

110. Kindness, is nothing more than an apology
for failure—a shared loss.

111. Looking at her & reaching into the
liquor cabinet, he exclaimed, "Must we make love?"

112. Manage ancestral memories; otherwise risk becoming a wasteland, half-bred.

113. "Jesus, man! what do you have running through your veins, sink water?" cried Edith.

114. Madness with originality is vision; without—merely borderline psychosis.

115. With European women, it is not just intellect, but cultural atmosphere as seduction.

116. You don't have a personal history, you only have dismissive data.

117. The internet is little more than a delusional exercise in 'Waiting for Godot'.

118. What is deep nostalgia, but a cloak thrown across ancient memory.

119. Worrying over one's mortality is a form of loneliness.

120. The definition of memory, is repetition, and that is why we forget.

121. Love is simply an apology for failures by which we attempt to humanise ourselves.

122. The definition of brilliance in any one person is this: Intense Honesty.

123. Post-structuralist abstraction in poetics is the refuge of less than mediocre talent.

124. I would rather be lost in Alaska than buried in New Zealand.

125. I wish I were self-righteous. Then I could believe in my own bullshit.

126. Guttural rumbling. Then thunder, and the rain gone up a notch, vertical falling.

127. When you combine the properties of Grief and Despair, you get Indifference.

128. It's all happening real fast now, it's like the off-ramp of a dream.

129. Being alive is like having free tickets to yourself—it's a spectacle.

130. Poets talk about what is missing, or gone, that is, momentary recognition.

131. The village idiot's smile was more a case of parting the face on either side.

132. Beauty is an accident with an inherent sense of design. Godless or not.

133. Fraught families born into a bad town feel at home. It's anonymity.

134. Main Street banner read: BRAIN INJURY AWARENESS WEEK. How'd you know?

135. New Zealand doesn't have funny stand-up comedians. It's not a funny country.

136. What else is right-wing populism but the fruit of excess and boredom.

137. Is lust merely an aberration of love, or is love nothing other than an apology for it?

138. Undercurrents of racism: one ethnic group against another—is the echo of evolution.

139. We've forgotten what it is to be part of the natural world. Rainfall is an abstraction.

140. Sudden sense of mortality first flared
off Neolithic cave wall paintings.

141. God save me from hipsters quagmired in
the present as a defensive rear-guard action.

142. Ghosts that exist in our minds are just
as real as those that do not.

143. Arachnids are property developers;
they know how to spin a yarn.

144. When definitions falter, and boundaries blur,
that is when the Visigoths move in.

145. If there's no God there's only a nothingness
of the constant moment.

146. That you do not believe in a god;
reach to a greater dignity to survive. No choice.

147. The grammatical archery of English
perception; Americans employ a slingshot approach.

148. Poets are haunted by their last draft; they
will sacrifice a relationship for it.

149. He lunged at her breasts, "Noli Me Tangere!"
screamed Edith.

150. Ego-obsessed, or solipsistic poetry
is nothing more than a tip-truck tumble of words.

151. And that is what revelation is, to make
an honest truth visible.

152. Stupid people are dishonest by birth;
nothing to do with learned behaviour.

153. Second-hand bookshops love poets.
They are the elephants' graveyard for poetry books.

154. Mortality is a cul-de-sac. And that is why we possess memory; it is an escape.

155. The mic-stand threw a garter shadow across her bare thigh, quaveringly.

156. A Cessna, at night, under cloud, falling like a mediaeval crucifix.

157. Arrowheads were invented by man through the study of birds in flight.

158. One cleave of the broadsword took head & shoulder both. Shield arm become his cradle.

159. There's nothing loud about the NZ bush, I mean, it ain't no lurid undergrowth.

160. The definition of controlled fantasy is science fiction.

161. Youth declares: I do what I want, therefore, I am who I am. A squabble of sparrows.

162. Global tension? The film industry and the pulpit depend upon it.

163. Personal anxieties are masks we adopt to distance ourselves from our realities.

164. Personal integrity supersedes worldly success—dissipates the illusion of it.

165. Christians were never given the choice to be pagans; the river of guilt runs deep.

166. I like graveyards old, mostly. You know where you stand, everyone knows their place.

167. Query: toss of a coin between anecdote & digression. Which one would win?

168. Very stupid people can be cleverly fucked in the head and you wouldn't know it.

169. If the inner skull holds the brain's imprint, does that mean text can read itself?

170. Sickle moon. Muslim moon. Boomerang moon. It cuts through with indifference.

171. Ascending her own personal crucifix—Heaven for her was an S&M dungeon.

172. Youth takes itself seriously; a question mark of doubt unfulfilled. Glorious expectation of loss.

173. Sky turned velvet, and rolling west, the Bill Henson gloom-set.

174. One of life's great pleasures is leaning against a farm gate—and she agreed.

175. "I am not out to impress anyone, expression is all about symmetry," stated Edith.

176. Depression Camps in the borderlands close by that hidden country called Elation.

177. He spun the chamber and asked, which came first the conviction or the image?

178. After the cat died she took to changing the flowers at her local church.

179. Without any knowledge of our ancient, deep past we are as straws in the wind.

180. One ponders the nature of instinct: do birds land on electric fences?

181. Surrealist moment, captured, but briefly. Diversity flatlines.

182. As Edith plummeted down the lift well she was heard to yell, "A plague on hipsters!"

183. A freeze-frame image is nothing other than over-taxed memory.

184. "I cannot wait to depart the planet," said the poet on his deathbed. "Free travel."

185. He was so paranoid reflected headlights freaked him out catatonically.

186. The psyche objectifying itself might be allied to the Depression of Indifference.

187. We live in the Age of Neo-Mediaevalism: rape, murder, terrorism on a global scale.

188. What is paranoia but a form of impatience; or something not happening as expected.

189. My mottoes: Don't believe it till it happens & you're only as good as your last job.

190. Political correctness is indicative of our mutual distrust of one another.

191. The Cult of Immediacy. Resist it if you are to preserve your individuality.

192. Women demand to be desired in order to enact the power of rejection.

193. The over-confident talk of an insecure man knows no punctuation.

194. What else were pirates in the roadstead but bikers of the seaways.

195. If history is the archaeology of spirit then it is also the DNA of memory.

196. Apparently, half a pound of hashish will knock over a six ton elephant.

197. People don't want truth, only personal endorsement of their own insecurities.

198. The contemporary mind: the seepage of the unconscious seeking out myth.

199. Death is a reminder that all expectations of life are futile.

200. The world's a talkfest. Everything means nothing. Tower of Babel. Babble of tongues.

201. As boundaries & conventions dissolve, we play hopscotch in the psychic minefield.

202. Hear the whistling winds of destruction—we've outbred our welcome on this planet.

203. Tonight, not yet full, the moon, bestowing its secrets of loss, burns silver.

204. Tomorrow doesn't exist. Live for the moment. That's where the action is.

205. The function of the dream world is to mythologize our doubts and fears.

206. I got pub-barred a lot—apparently, my crime was in constructing a complete sentence.

207. That big Ol' full moon, ain't it like a train light coming hard at you!

208. The Epoch of Indulgence is over. Industrial Age via neoliberalism. Covid saw to that.

209. Communication now is all too immediate. There is no time for reflection.

210. I am beginning to think that the human race has contracted a collective death-wish.

211. Spent my life reading great literature, writing poems, womanising & getting drunk.

212. NZ doesn't have a National Rifle Association, it has Federated Farmers instead.

213. If I remember correctly—drunkenness is self-imposed Alzheimer's.

214. The Sisyphus myth embodies Sartre's 'passion Inutile'—endless struggle, no gain.

215. I enjoy seeing couples holding hands. Configures the big M for marriage. Good luck!

216. "What else could love possibly be but shared vulnerability," lamented Edith.

217. I will find the numinous anywhere and without self-contradiction.

218. And then, Noah said, "The Lord told me there will be climate change."

219. What is acceptance of self but the transition from failure to belief.

220. We superimpose emotional values upon sex. Incorrect. It is simply a biological act.

221. If women understand the intentions of men can they forgive them?

222. The secret to happiness is simple, you've just got to outlive the arseholes.

223. The one thing that ambition is afraid of—is originality, because it exposes falsehood.

224. The measure of a dishonest man is his flattery.
You just have to recognise it.

225. And after the first interrogation he said,
"I drink to exhaust my demons."

226. My mind is my book. Translate thought.
Artistic expression follows.

227. It is charm that protects the vulnerability of
women. In these times, a lost art.

228. If a nuclear explosion lit up the horizon at dusk
would birds fly to it?

229. Some birds & bats emit calls
at a sonic frequency we can't hear. So does thought.

230. It is not death we fear, only the threat of eternal
forgetfulness.

231. Is there anything original in my thought—
or is that loneliness? I do not know.

232. Every cloud structure—is the riddle of that
conversation one never had.

233. The dignity of the mind presupposes the
existence of a god. Hope v futility.

234. Beware the procrustean edicts of university
writing courses. One bed fits all.

235. On the ramparts of pride to attack oneself with
negativity is to admit defeat.

236. I think love is (or should be) the recognition
of truth between two people.

237. To be truly crazy, you have to know exactly
what you are doing.

238. So long as we're comfortable within our own insecurities & endorsed, who cares?

239. One is permitted to be attractive when young—it entitles you to be irresponsible.

240. If the Roman Empire had not existed would the Christ figure have prevailed?

241. His eyelids campsites but her legs looked honest. He spun the chamber again. The End.

242. Friendship is synonymous with trust, you can't have one without the other.

243. Material & supernatural worlds cannot coexist within the same space-time continuum.

244. In order to be powerful, one must be delusional; I am defeated by my own honesty.

245. A good poem always hangs in the balance—like a tightrope walker over the chasm.

246. The greatest unwritten law of the universe is for parents to protect their children.

247. "Goddam ain't it always the way ambushed in my own bathroom," wailed Edith.

248. The only thing that is more self-defeating than paranoia is indifference.

249. A poet, in order to be great, must first be deprived of light—then see it.

250. There is absolutely no end to the universe. It is just waiting for us to catch up.

251. Families are, in essence, forced friendships; you don't know who you can trust.

252. What is it to survive? Survival is the recognition of loss.

253. Paddocks beige as Afghanistan amidst a Taliban of turkeys. Drought.

254. Every poem is an expression of guilt. Believe in it—in order to be acquitted.

255. To exist on the periphery of genius, cried the clown, tumbling through a fire hoop.

256. The object of genius is to supersede what we know—unknowingly.

257. In the Beginning was Lust. And Laughter fell upon the face of the Earth.

258. Originality is heightened honesty by which memory is validated.

259. Clarity of thought & clarity of perception —are declensions of literary style.

260. "What he lacks in mind," argued the defence lawyer, "he makes up in mimicry."

WELCOME GHOST

The curtained light through bird's wings.
            River takes the sky with it,
sun tight-rope walks a spider's web.

Then clouds, and an explosive white, falling,
            awaits the sun sinking.

            Pine cones bunched as birds
on branches. Ritual is the residue of memory.

Fireworks, deep-buried in the sky's cavern,
hieroglyphic, blazed against the dark,
            curved-walled multiverse.

            Tail of a comet,
longer than a prayer; God's fingernail
tearing time.
            Belief-systems, buoyant
as cork, tossed either side.

Twilight, the contained rumble of wheelie
bins announce the advent of a new work-week.

            Film is the manifestation of
reflection qua dream, as it subsides into
the 'Well of Forgetfulness'—memory, muted.

            A smoky Ol' moon atop
the ridgeline of an apartment block, hinting
at autumn, welcome ghost.

An electric scooter in the half-light,
leaf bobbing at the fence line like a rat's head,
darkening into dusk.

You wouldn't dream about it, in a vision,
the psychic lighthouse keeper captures the next
rung trapezing, silver haloed.

      Bucket of light from an anvil
cloud, spilling—sundown, a molten lake.

Branches shoulder back and forth against
a layabout wind.

Pylons and low slung lines slouch
and stretch hills. A regimen of spectral trees,
     translucent, a dusty yellow.

Camellia bloom, a mosaic of snowflake,
deepens autumn—the drawbridge of winter,
    darkly looming.

Sunset withdraws into watercolour.
Another day done—now for the portal.

     Late autumn leaves
flock and regroup. A few stragglers make it
over the grassy knoll.

Swallows drop, traverse totara stands,
steadfast, in a hollow dip.
     Orini District Church;
terra cotta roof tiles, pale brown, lit brick.

         The marble plaque states:
'This stone was laid on 10 September 1955.'
A functional, roadside rest stop.

Sunset calibrates its alignment, and tilts—
core drills an icy cloudbank.
Rows of poplars make x-rays of themselves.

O the gift that destroys—
leaf-stripped trees promulgate autumn;
upended, witches brooms.
Soon, the low thrum of winter trees.

         The wait,
submarine cloud surfacing into moonrise,
and as you enter the cave of recall—
stillness, indrawn breath, exhalation.

SWING BRIDGE

The pitch-down slumbering of wind amongst that
stand of radiata pine, while closer, the flung rattle-

tattle of leaves off hollowed branches of a tree
I could not name of a common enough species this

side of the gully, and the creak and gentle rock
of the swing bridge, beneath which a thin stream

loosely scrolled its signature. Meanwhile, a twist
of iron-cables tautly contained each tremulation airily,

with each step forward or taken back, through
autumn, its lungs full, breathing easy. Only a mother

and a baby filled pram—one child running ahead
down the narrow planking of the bridge, she content

within her domestic bubble, apart and untroubled,
a wished for simplicity, that came and went.

UNWRITTEN

Mountains are the homeland of winter.
Cities are caves where we leave our memories,
materializing into holograms buzzing a
Neanderthal encampment.

        Light that flicked (you)
ahead. Shadowy anger of an extinct hominin
species tracks us yet, reverberates from

the deep well of the unconscious, lost along
migratory paths—vistas subsumed to
algorithms of dreamscape, ritual and recall;
that very act of incision is a recording.

It is a long way back to that old laughter,
still fresh on those windless, hapless days, long
since buried, then recalled.

        It is a long way back
to some beige-glazed roadside paddock, high
summer, and the far off bark of an unseen dog,
the heat, emptiness ahead and behind.

It is a long way to those spirits the darkness
calls forth, either expectantly, or uninvited, that
swim in airy currents about you or in stillness.

        It is a long way back
to the poem which lurks, unwritten and fugitive,
slowly forming, urged through your mind,

that emerges as hooded figure on the dark
road—caught in the lantern glare of your gaze,
his form falling into focus, as you advanced.

THE CARETAKER

What do I own if ownership is nothing,
and if nothing holds, what holds me?

      The shamanic embrace says
acceptance is denial, that survival is the
measure and tread of time.

Car lights strobe under guttering where
the TV armature is a rowing eight.

I am the caretaker of absence,
sweeper over empty skies, scuffing cloud
into scruffy piles—

      from one corner of the day
to the next, endlessly, but without end,

down through the corridors of twilight,
on windless days or windy.

Small, airy dramas, with the harrier hawk
wheeling, nonchalantly, out-of-reach,

      above the diving and angling
magpie, diminished in size against that
raptor's wingspan—nesting in a

macrocarpa beneath, beyond farmgate,
in the chill autumn air, play out
before the green arena unfolding beyond.

WHAT LIES AHEAD

Dull thump upon the wall is not the ruffling of
any bookshelf. Partial cloud and a rough-hewn moon.

The misguided hope guides us away, to hell
and back, the belief questioned, and the habit lost.

Belief stretched on the rack of unbelief—silence
of the scream, though not the scream itself.

Memory distorts, caught in the rear-guard action
of doubt and dare. I stomp over the graveyard of my

youth, while beauty retires, lizard-like, under its rock.
A straight line is what lies ahead, where the world

flatlined before the tilt over the edge into an eternal
waterfall, soundless—swirling mime of other worldly

wings, dissolution of memory left behind, become
that which lies above, overhead, and earthly.

The wind will make of those branches violin bows;
whatever remains unsaid, taunts, and in its twisting,

is uncapturable. Bunkered in the anteroom of our
dreams, amongst childhood terrors, within the cessation

of time, and therefore, half-formed, yet disconnected—
finally, dissolved upon waking. A stillness, momentarily

flat as concrete before instinct struggles upright,
ultimately diffused upon the first exhalation of dawn.

RUIN

Cattle clustered on a hilltop, around the farmstead,
fly-speck distant. Next paddock, one brown and white cow

taking a stance, an impressionistic portrait to be painted.
Man of the land in sync with the seasons, conspicuously

absent. Long blades of grass bent to the light in rivulets
cascade the slope. With the seasons, there is hardly any

shadow of doubt. What else, but the parting curtain,
and spring. Face masks of cloud wrap around the horizon,

and breathe rain. The day falls to ruin, dissolves into an
archaeological dig of recollection silent, still as dirt.

The reflection of language upon truth, which is the one
deflecting off the other without fault, can be heartless,

because it is as unalterable as it is undeniable to a fault;
our questioning guides us backward and forward

steady as a heartbeat or the slow palpitations which rise
up into fully fledged phantoms untrustworthy as doubt.

Love then, an image projected onto the lake's surface—
dissolving, what emerges as after-image is simulacrum.

The slipstream of memory frays, becomes soundless
as regret, a puppet show that is mime or remembrance.

SHUTTERS

After Tony Hoagland

She told me, after I paid by card, collected my bottle
of red from the liquor store door (Covid level 3 lockdown)

muffled through her mask, "He said to me," she confided
in mock surprise, "You don't seem to do much here."

To which she replied, "You don't know the shit I have to
put up with." If strung out she didn't show it.

                On the path outside the Bin Inn (and Post
Office) a guy sits and holds up a cardboard sign that pleads

for food and money, who then as quickly walks
away when a hooded woman appears and takes his place

in a coordinated, business arrangement to maximize
returns, a practised gesture of bargain basement begging.

                Thoughts bang shut like shutters in a high
wind, slide to neutral as you turn the key in the ignition

and head back to your solitary unit, toward the nest of
dysfunctional neighbours, their low life, freeloading lives.

                I cope with this by imagining them
as extras in a Federico Fellini movie, grotesque figures,

behind roped off barriers, gormless, scratching bodies, staring
gape-mouthed at the beautiful heroine whose incandescence

goads them to animal shrieks and grunts, before the trucks
herd them back into the grimy, smoke-filled ghettos.

This transports me out of the neighbourhood for a while,
assisted by the bottle of red now sunk to a low Plimsoll line.

The following day, around midmorning, I will seek out
a back road farmgate to lean on and converse with the clouds.

THE PRINTER

for John Denny

There is something military about letterpress machines. They sit stolid and grounded, quiet as field guns in the no-man's land of the imagination, tempered and trained to respond under the guiding hand of the printer. Type selected and balanced upon fingertips, set letter by letter, word by word.

Press of the lever on quality cream paper stock. Conclusive, repeated click of machinery wheels. It speaks its own language. Meanwhile, the world outside the printer's shed hums and computes its obscurantist algorithms, oblivious to the press and bite of type, page after page.

Spring unfolds, hand stitching leaves to trees. What is it heard here, felt within the breath of machinery steadfastly at work, but the concordant and forgotten dialogue of horse hooves and carts over cobbled ways, rain punctuating slate roofs, a distant bell ringer, the lighting of gas lamps.

But then there is the slightest, barely audible hush of paper sheets that grow and gather into a stack, an exhalation of the printing press, telling of creaking sails at the inlet, faint piano notes issuing from an upper room of some long-lost village manor, fingers turning the newly printed page—while elsewhere, in dingy attics, the proclaimed manifestos of poets, artists, revolutionaries.

DIGITAL GHOSTS

On the decimation of World Literature extirpated from the NZ National Library.

The sparrow and the bumble bee—the pea-green boat is the mandarin tree. Bumble bee with a full hull, drops down, turns starboard. One sparrow. A shadow. One sparrow, singing 'threepence' repeatedly, hammering a piano key, flashing inside its head. On to the next branch. Closer. Not a tweet.

You could be looking from a cherry picker right inside that tree. The song remains the same. You think about that for a bit by which time it's gone. 'Minutiae' calls the blackbird announcing dusk. I agree, the whole thing shut down. Rain, steady as a slow train passing. 'She wants to be pretty, she wants to be liked' you surmise of the couple passing by the other side of the wooden fence.

Can an incident avoided yet be an introduction or is it nothing other than the crossing of boundaries? The truck and trailer units arrive under cover of dark. Shadowy figures lifting crates of books off the landing bay into the containers to be shipped out like overstayers. Scanned, then dumped into a mass graveyard of second hand bookshops or remote warehouses in the Mojave Desert under lock & key.

Hear the muffled voices subside into dusty silence. First editions become coffins for the voices of long dead authors. Two dimensional entities wailing round forlorn mesas and through the empty shelves. Digital ghosts extracted from the printed page, reduced to the muted babble of tongues, and memory the last, fading note of the songbird, dissolving in the twilight at the end of an era.

October 31, 2021

FARTHER OFF

Tesserae of Suffolk sheep. Even at this angle, difficult to count. A handful at best—the paddock opposite the cantilevered cranes, foundational, iron-caged reinforcing, yellow and orange tip trucks strewn about the riverside, a child's overturned toy box. And I, on the other side here at the lookout, river sweep indifferently flexing past. Bridge span under construction, slowly falling into place. And I, seeing the whole thing through time-lapse photography. The Meccano methodically assembling. Autopsy in reverse.

Soon enough, grid-locked houses will arise ghostly as boxed fungi. Diffuse light spillage. One pill-popping moon. Intermittent keyboard of bird species trebling through high wind in oak trees. That is farther off still, can only be defined as memory. Nothing is complete, can only be defined as regret. Hope is absence. It is where one is—isolated on the viewing deck of consciousness threading across plains, deserts and horizons, muffled into mountain passes. Thought envisioned as wild horses in full flight before the footfall of mesas that stud Utah. Cloud rush. Stammer of chopper blades.

LOOKOUT

'Curtsey Girls' I call them, wide hems, drip
lines all in a row, three small, bunched trees front
onto the expressway.

           A stream the colour of shit,
under the viaduct, creeps by. Paddocks green as the
Promised Land. You could be anywhere.

Clouds still as brake pads. A lingering heat
and hideaway sun. Uapoto Road, farmgate lookout;
Pirongia, Kakepuke, Maungatautari—blurred.

Irrigation sprinklers (wash out from cow sheds),
lassoing pastures. The wide sweep of hills crouched
in shadowy ambush.

Flatlands as landing strips for afternoon light.
The choral wind up of cattle lowing. A fence line
disappearing straight as a rifle shot.

           Senate of myna birds bombasting
as the oaken grove thickens; the seasonal takeover
near complete.

The world's tapestry, and your place in it, only
silence married unto stillness, that timeless corridor
through which you may now pass.

COMPASS

I wish I could go back, just to see, be reminded
for a moment, when the first envisioning of word
into shadowy light told me I was a poet, and so
I continue to seek out that fleeting moment, but on
approach, it bounds out of view like a jack rabbit,
one poem chasing upon the next.

               A small clearing in the
entanglement of childhood perhaps, floating there,
some guiding spirit, barely recognized though
sensed. An inner compass, an orchestrated journey,
seeking out the known within the unknown.
Processional dance of twilight ghosts who emerge,
then diminish. Vigil and loneliness that haunt,
those necessary companions lying in wait to set
the stage for ambush.

BURN DOWN THE AMAZON

Burn down the Amazon. Move the cattle in. Don't worry. McDonald's will buy the meat. Amazon burgers & fries this week's special. Burn down the Amazon. Plant soybean. Shave the land bare. Dig it up. Dry it out. Turn the green and emerald into grey. Who needs it? But what is that gasping you hear, did you imagine it? See how the trees recoil, retreat in shock before the shriek of chainsaws, the ground-breaking growl of bulldozers. Rip down the trunks, they'll reinvent themselves as coffee tables. Burn down the Amazon far as the eye can see, and further still.

What is that pile of ash, was that an indigene's dwelling? Brazil buckles under Bolsonaro's iron heel. Each morning he scrawls in his black book, 'Progress is wealth. Clear-cut trees as far as the eye can see.' *Quema el Amazonas* tattooed on his wrist. But look out! Here come the ghosts rising above the canopy like mist, swarming from the dark. They are deadly. They are silent. They contain memories of all the birdsong wiped clean off the slate—out of the Amazon. Your ears will ring though you will hear nothing within the reign of nothingness. Dead dreams as far as the eye can see, and further still. Taste the dead air. Yes, there is nothing else for it. Burn down the Amazon.

November 27, 2021

FANDANGO

for Nicholas Birns

One bird memories another in a flock of thought, the musicality winding up in the orchestra pit of trees—pushing around reality like a Frank O'Hara poetic caper, cavorting in a collapsing fandango for all or none to hear and see. His breath the suction and cushioning, close of a studio door, the mind soundproofed, the poem recorded in voluble breath and sufflation.

Oh how he hopes that nothing is lost or is forever! In the process of doing so. Such exhalations and dismissals! Those coloured cubes of words tossed airily, the fusillade of multiple doubts offset, drowned out, in that cacophonous dismantling the machinery of language.

Stalactites are the monster cave's mouth, dark tongue stretching back down the fossilised highway, echoes shaping the footprints and wall's low hum, forgotten dialogues before the bone-crack of fire roar, bulk of night sky pushing aside the snaggle-toothed cave entrance. Read the dictionary of star wobble watching shadow-stealth. River bed rambunctious water flow. What proposals by firelight! What exaltations rune at the back of the skull waiting to be unlocked millennia hence, resting there bookended by cliff face and lamplight.

December 5, 2021

OBLIGATORY

'I am even disallowed the freedom to be successful.' He had scrawled on the breath-frosty windowpane. Every great perception of any one writer, that transcendent leap—is a trap for another. The still point and revelation. As instantaneous as loss; that which is understood, an invitation refused but, nevertheless, observed. Nothing is ever discarded, abandoned, but seeks safety in the harbour of the subconscious, beyond immediate detection and rides the roadstead, that ultimately of all its failures, turns triumphant.

Again, he scrawled on the breath-chilled pane, 'The endless summer days of my youth. O autumnal relationships.' Nothing lasts. One can only shadow existence. What the object, what the shadow? That there is no God—only endlessness. All else is obligatory distraction. That we live in order to die. 'Explanation is meaningless.' He ghostily wrote. In one recurrent dream he opens the slide doors of an upper story apartment, steps out onto the balcony. Sees the fidgeting lights of the fading traffic flow below, the city under open heart surgery. No need to leap within the confines of failure, yet gravity gripped him as though falling.

YOU SEE IT

What crime—we make our gestures,
don't we? In order to envision.

      We spend half our lives
asking questions. There are no answers,
only how you see it. It's nothing.

      Transposition into the thing
itself, that sounds like a holy communion,
reflectively.

      Every observation is a map.
See you there, and thanks, always
an 'epistle to self'. The lost gospel, folks!

Sky unfolds like papyri, Deserts are honest.
The quiet of the dissolving footprint.

Sort of a light grinding 'shush' strongly in
need of some life-affirming libation.

      Every breath is a new thought.
If only we could know. If only it were so,
we would recognize such ghosts.

      For ghosts, indeed, they are!
And yes, they are seen, playing
rollerball within our minds, our hearts.

In sleep, they are absent.
If only sleep were allowed. Sleep casting

      its time-honoured reprieve, one step back—

          to crystal blue retsina, peculiar
to Naxos, there amongst the scent

of thyme, elevated before the sweep
of the Cyclades, December, 1979, white

outcrops of marble, high up on that island,
      the wild poppy bloom aglow.

I've thought about it over the years,
or rather, the thought has pursued me.
      The lockdown question of love

      which I equate with loss, so much
then for melancholy, a broken down dream,
taste of fleeting memory that recalls it.

      Caught, the last truckload dump
of twilight shred through leaves, branches,
come 7:30 PM or thereabouts.

      Looked like an imprint of some
sluice gate you'd never seen before.

      The structure that's left behind,
memory snapped, before you got
there, then gone. Filigreed off under

      water vapour, by the headland,
before thought breakers intruded repeatedly.

Does instinct run backwards to what was
        not, tracing the chalk outline,

        life an unresolved crime scene,
the detective breakdown of your
past, the way it once was or imagined?

And she considered a lady of great
        presence and beauty arisen from
the Bronze Age.

Not now, another dream devolving,
one half sliced moon bleeding light—
        within its aureole opalescent.

Pressure crush on gravel roads,
        our belief systems turned to dust.

GRAND TOUR

A conversation with the self is always an engagement with 'the other', the undisclosed identity, its presence made evident by the anonymity of the question, nascent as sense before thought—never asked. 'To whom do I address myself?' Perhaps this is the guide leading us through the sensory terrain out of childhood's enclosure. The gate shut behind, and that which must not be remembered, never will. We cannot know 'the other' ever, because it is always ahead of us, indeterminate steps, but always beyond reach, and when we stop, so too this guardian or guide, that reminds us we are on a grand tour, perhaps uninvited yet somehow, or in part, belonging. Travelling over suspected terrain, though unfamiliar, which I suppose for that very reason is endless, as we pursue those shadows in passing, wondering what we have missed.

GRID

A sense of it. Feeling and loss—
is that how it ends; honesty, the limp
flag of surrender, to what?

      The hedge chopping chatter
of sparrows.

Or: Bedouin love knots tied to
branches of acacia trees, an acoustic,
rock amphitheatre, Sinai desert,
silence so deep you hear it.

      That which has been spoken,
before or after.

Night, the lava flow of traffic
fills city grids, laid out flatly below,
horizon wide and far. The year
intersects, subsides to a halt.

Falling figure from a parapet
belongs to daydreams that stalk you
through precipitate sleep.

      Invisible talons stretch
from here to the moon.

In this dreamscape, fantasy has
replaced belief, in all its multifarious
incarnations; defaced road signage
leads nowhere—destiny a dead end.

FAR OFF

Each circumstance differed in that a woman
you otherwise knew, maybe the same physical
person, though not the same as she seemed
at another location, in some far-off country, or
that you had shifted in or out, at some other
remove; she already become memory, so too
undoubtedly, you to her. But even here you
were not privy to the moment, nor wished to be.
Somehow, you had both removed yourselves
from each other into something as yet undefined
or undisclosed, not quite strangers yet, though
you could never be completely that, emotions
safeguarded within an anonymity by which
you came to identify each other, apart from
each other, a manufactured indifference devoid
of even passing sentiment. Small changes
inherited from each, the barest of recognitions,
beyond lingering sadness or desire recalled.
And the heart pulling back upon dismantled,
sunken memories, held within that chain locker.

DEAD RINGER

British stamps from between the wars,
suffused with the reds of dying sunsets, faded
greens of forgotten countryside, amber
light off oaken panels seen dissolving through
the decorous counties of *Foyle's War*;
royal blue (two toned, with black mudguards)
or coal red paintwork of period automobiles,
the stylish trilby, hardly as rakish as the Chicago
or New York variety, nor the wearer so brash.
This is, after all, genteel English behaviour
of the '40s. Murder most foul remains, if not a
mystery, nevertheless, an abrupt and brutal
act, the hinge, like the brass hinged office doors,
through which decisions pass, upon which
everything devolves. Nostalgia is the happy face
we put on to disguise the protocols of loss.
The street procession. The shaky litter. The plaster
saint that teeters toward the cathedral square,
and villagers ambling at a leisurely pace—
something of the moon in its death mask stare.

Yet, to walk in the 'empire of shadows'—
ancestor worship, schizophrenia, hallucination.
O you can't fake time. 'Suppose', 'suppose',
once was, Wyatt Earp, 'the town-taming Marshal'
original 'beat' who as a young man bore a
singular likeness to Rupert Brooke, dead ringer
(go figure). 'Hell on Wheels' shantytowns
sprung up—Tombstone in advance of the Union
Pacific Rail (Old West) where 'men of every shade
and character' worked the silver mines. Earp,
whorehouse bouncer, coach guard, turned lawman,
branded an outlaw (shunned) back on the trail,
reputation more or less intact, but the truth never
told, dogged him, 'old sins cast long shadows'
into his sunset years. Earp didn't get to set
the record straight when alive; 'suppose', 'suppose',
whispered to (wife) Josephine on his deathbed,
but mythmakers had the last word. The End.

SHE WATCHES

One solitary, Turkish woman, looking
out through the meshed, screen door of her
home, silhouette still, a tessellated mosaic.
She watches, menfolk dismantle dwellings,
saving what they can, lumber, windows,
support beams, house fittings.

      The Birecik Dam now completed
as the Euphrates slowly rises to flood
this village. She has lived here her whole
life, the children grown and married.
Memory darkens to shadow. She watches,
what once was, now ruins, mud walls,
partitions, tumbling into the rising waters.

As though she had forgotten she was
once young, eyes light-filled as the night
sky, how love waited, but this could
not survive beyond innocence, her fabled
histories reduced to rubble—old age,
yearning for that which no longer exists.

TREMORS

With Jack Gilbert, living on Paros
or Santorini, it was the freedom to let go,
trust his reach, wherever it took him;
houses tumbling like white dice seaward.
A simple thing, the beauty in the space
he got to defeat emptiness. My memories
float as kites back to the Cyclades, lapis
lazuli waters. Here, lip-smacking tar,
summer hot, asphalt roads. Heat mirages
dissolving off into distances. Out of sight,
over the river bend, sunset is a sunken
shipwreck within this southern archipelago.
Somehow, the tide of old friendships had
retreated way back from the shoreline of
some other self, and the tremors not yet
felt, of its seismic return—the horizon
steadfast as a spirit level, reassuring in the
way stillness is, when not a warning.

OSSUARY

for Gary Mutton

Not quite midsummer. Already, beige, tide rolling hills through January. Bluely, the seismic ridgeline of Pirongia mountain rising into dusk. The river below capturing constellations, continuously, shift downstream. That people are elsewhere, not here—nor within the reach of atmospherics. What happens is expected. Shuttle service of day into night.

Expectation pounces back in time or not at all. How much of this is willed, wishes atrophied or turned to dust. Only small epiphanies remain, preserved within the ossuary of peculiar silence, the other side of every elusive moment. Doubt is always residue, and memory never transformative, an uninvited waiting. So, too, ghosts, costumed and recalled, fleetingly.

He told me how he had disappeared into the state forest. Endless serried ranks of pine. A dream of suburban houses. But for the moment, here they stood, straight as soldiers, staunch guardians. You might conclude, he was the one human wilding amongst them. Maybe the daily carolling of magpies for company and at night, the creak of branches while winds waffled through tree tops, spearheading stars. His reasons for flight largely fugitive, though a necessary escape in his van along the firebreak, then deeper into the forest. At least for now, safely beyond the reach of the harridan. A sanctuary of sorts, isolated, but not lonely.

REBRANDED FREEDOM

An uprooted tree after the storm cordoned off resembles a crime scene. 150 mph wind gusts burgling branches. The harried, nor-east getaway. The suburb looking like a shattered bird's nest. The unseen roar all night long. Vision is a reminder, it is an urging.

One white painted statue of the Christ figure standing before the Catholic church, arms spread wide, raised in the manner of a conductor, orchestrating the cosmos, and a world eternally fallen.

The seemingly endless flow, a habit of living, the big and small concerns like wagons arranged in a circle about our prospects at any given moment. But all that vanished with the global virus, everyone masked like bandits. No one able to roam the planet freely any longer.

Protests and illegal encampments. Blockades. People lamenting the loss of luxuries once taken for granted. Things not needed considered essentials for comfort. Expediency. Short term demands governed by short term memory. Consumerism as entitlement. A mixed bag of contradictory wants. Banners and flag waving. Contagion of selfishness rebranded freedom.

He goes to one of his two river lookouts. This one by the heritage mansion with its turret. He looks down the bushy slope to the path visible between the greenery then over the river, myriad ripples of sunlight passing in stillness. He is never overly bothered—cars parked further on down the road where the kids leap off the pier. But here he is left alone mostly.

The patient river flow emptying his mind. The city beyond the bank on the other side unseen. He sees terraced apartments with glassed in decking. The one remaining old wooden building with its three, snug balconies sitting grandly just below the ridgeline. An invitation to solitude beyond reach.

ENACTED ELSEWHERE

'Because nothing is left,' he wrote, 'myths are reduced to brand names and labels on supermarket shelves. Division the one thing we all have in common. Politicians and priests—spruikers cut from the same cloth.' No aerial bombardment other than what starlight might manage in the countryside. Meanwhile, within the city, concrete barriers remain in place. The barbed wire leer of the protestors on the other side confronting the police line. Slogans and banners of conspiracy theorists. The endless wait for something or nothing to happen in the push and pull of anger.

Even under the 'variegated English elm' in the public gardens. Or any other tree in its pool of shadow. Exercising his eyes over the flickering leaves, and stillness all around him in the greenness held there like a secret. Memory is a riot enacted elsewhere. Then there is that other emptiness, the cacophony of hurt though not recognized as such, buried within the panacea of pettiness or distraction rising to a kettledrum clash and crescendo. But nothing is heard in the muted clamour of the crowd. In the imagining of it.

And then he remembers the dawn walk up the mountainside from the harbour cafes and bars below on Hydra. Everything emerging—from a negative slowly coming into focus. The Norwegian pointing out to him the grainy rust stain from the guttering running down the whitewashed wall, its crystalline translucence, something only a Scandinavian would first notice, something that Tomas Tranströmer delicately netted time and time again.

PHANTOMS

The smallest things are not only acutely perceived in detail but amplified in loneliness. We are each of us a universe unto ourselves. The lone poet, seeking himself out, lonesome, in company—is both a hiding and an escape. Oft-times wrapped in the safety of some far-flung recollection. Colourful stills of childhood. Youth's mosaic. The lost wonders.

A late summer afternoon coming home from school, my mother lying on a blanket, face down on a pillow, asleep, in the angling sun. A woman's magazine and Capstan Plain cigarettes nearby. 'Out-the-back' of our Karepa Street home, by the weatherboard bach, next to the passionfruit vine that never fruited, strangling the slumped summerhouse with an old park seat no one ever sat on. Stillness of the declining day with the sun heading westward. Backdrop to the ramshackle hen house and run, its few peach trees gone to wood, then further back still to the towering macrocarpa, where the morepork called softly from the top of the tree late into the night, though never seen. All of which no longer exists. Phantoms materializing on the photoplate of memory.

LONG SINCE ENDED

Wake of a riverboat ribbons out shoreward on this
or any other day. Primordial forest beyond dreamscape,
long since perished, partially glimpsed, ghosted the
mind. Had he ever been in love, or merely longed
for it, adventure turned disastrous, two lives drowned
in the net's entanglement? Decides he should never
have come back to the familiar, or seen from a train
window across a new country for the first time, jolts
memory of what he cannot determine or give shape to,
lingers momentarily. He wonders if this was meant
for him, something other intercepted, headed elsewhere.
What are ghosts after all but unfinished sentences,
relationships gone bad, long since ended but neither
had the courage to admit it, the way ahead less certain,
more a holding pattern than the journey undertaken.

DUCK ISLAND

There is a small island one side of the river,
close in to the shore, back from the stone stepped
embankment. An elevated water pipe on pylons
runs through to the treatment plant up ahead.
A narrow sweep of river, stilled, reaches between
the shore and Duck Island. Seats facing up river
along the walkway to the public gardens, the
island seen middle distance. One scrappy bush
consuming about a third of it. Maybe islet might be
more exact. An elderly man sitting there alone
looking toward it. I say to him, "Imagine camping
on that island overnight." He responds quietly,
"The river would be black." Then he gets up and
walks away. That one remark alone made of
him a painter or poet, silence deep within him.

A NOTE ABOUT THE AUTHOR

Stephen Oliver—Australasian poet of fifteen poetry collections, seven chapbooks, and one memoir. Travelled extensively. Signed on with the radio ship *The Voice of Peace 1540 kHz* broadcasting in the Mediterranean out of Jaffa, Israel in the late '70s. Free-lanced in Australia/New Zealand as *production voice, narrator, newsreader, radio producer, columnist, copy and feature writer, etc*. Lived in Australia for 20 years. Currently living in NZ. He has published widely in international literary journals. Long-time contributor of creative non-fiction and poems to *Antipodes: A Global Journal of Australian/ New Zealand Literature*. Poems translated into German, Spanish, Chinese, and Russian. Represented most recently in the following: *Writing To The Wire Anthology*, edited by Dan Disney and Kit Kelen, University of Western Australia Publishing 2016; *The Australian Prose Poem Anthology*, edited by Cassandra Atherton and Paul Hetherington, Melbourne University Press 2020; *Poetry New Zealand Yearbook*, edited by Tracy Slaughter, Massey University Press 2021.

www.ingramcontent.com/pod-product-compliance
Lightning Source LLC
Chambersburg PA
CBHW030301010526
44107CB00053B/1768